ON COON MOUNTAIN

ON COON MOUNTAIN

*Scenes from a Childhood
in the Oklahoma Hills*

By
Glen Ross

University of Oklahoma Press : Norman and London

By Glen Ross

The Last Campaign: A Novel of Korea (New York, 1962; 1965)
On Coon Mountain: Scenes from a Childhood in the Oklahoma Hills
(Norman, 1992)

Library of Congress Cataloging-in-Publication Data
Ross, Glen, 1929–
    On Coon Mountain: scenes from a childhood in the Oklahoma
hills / by Glen Ross. — 1st ed.
      p. cm.
    ISBN 0-8061-2405-9 (alk. paper)
    1. Ross, Glen, 1929–   —Biography—Youth. 2. English
teachers—United States—Biography. 3. Authors, American—
20th century—Biography. 4. Oklahoma—Social life and cus-
toms. I. Title.
PE64.R67A3   1992
420′.71′173—dc20
[B]   91-29392
                                            CIP

The paper in this book meets the guidelines for permanence and du-
rability of the Committee on Production Guidelines for Book Longevity
of the Council on Library Resources, Inc. ∞

CONTENTS

ON COON MOUNTAIN

1 WAUHILLAU ("WHERE EAGLES NEST")

I WAS BORN in the house above the gray bluff on Coon Mountain, in what was once the Indian Territory, during a thunderstorm on the seventh of August, 1929. I had no choice in the matter; but if I had been consulted I might not have agreed to the terms, because the years that followed were years of calamity.

My father had to drive to town to get the doctor on that sultry August afternoon—rattling along at a bone-jolting thirty miles an hour in his 1929 Chevy. In the rearview mirror he could see black storm clouds rising over the mountain, and the chance of a cloud-burst sending the creeks out of their banks and cutting him off from home would have weighed on his mind. He wasn't a man to take things lightly, and he distrusted the weather more than anything in the world. But he also distrusted cars, and doctors, and the government; so he might have felt he was running a gauntlet of the fates.

The fourteen-mile trip never took less than an hour. The single-lane road wound through muddy hollows and over flint ridges so rough that when he tried to press on more speed the car would shudder and go into convulsions that shook the pipe right out of his mouth. But whatever awful scenes his creative anxiety cooked up that day remained only possibilities, for he was back home with the doctor before the storm broke, and my mother got such help as a doctor could provide under the circumstances. So did I. My certificate of birth shows that in compliance with what must have been a state law, the doctor put a drop of silver nitrate solution in each of my eyes—for which I thanked him politely, no doubt.

Having done that, the doctor washed his hands of me and went back to town, leaving me out there in the woods at the mercy of the natives. They were total strangers to me, and being unable to speak their language I could only guess at their intentions. Judging by the looks they gave me, I feared they were cannibals. When I was made to understand that they were all relatives of mine and that they had been expecting me, I was much relieved. It was a strange coincidence, to be sure, but a lucky one for me. I have been lucky with people all my life.

I had no idea where I was, however, or what I was supposed to be doing there. I didn't know that the year was 1929. To judge by the accomodations it could well have been 1829—a great year to be born—but my luck didn't run that way. It turned out to be the twentieth century, with droughts, depressions, and wars in every direction. Because I arrived when I did, I was seen as a contributory cause of those things by my father. He even suspected me of having something to do with the collapse of the stock market, which happened a few weeks after I was born. He never came right out and accused me of causing it, but I was a perceptive infant and could usually tell what was going through his mind.

On the whole I was well treated. The winter of 1929–30 was the coldest ever to afflict that part of the country, but nobody as much as hinted that I was to blame. In January the temperature at Watts—a few miles north of Coon Mountain—fell to twenty-seven degrees below zero. That was too cold for comfort, especially since our house wasn't finished yet. It had wood clapboards on the outside, but the inside had only canvas nailed across the studs without any sheetrock or insulation. There was a fireplace in the front room and a wood-burning cookstove in the kitchen. No plumbing or electricity. My only brother was two and a half years old that winter, and I was five months. I have been told that I didn't cry much as an infant, probably because I had prepared for the cold weather so well that I weighed eleven pounds at birth.

If this is so, it shows more foresight than I have since been able to account for.

In spite of the disadvantages of being born poor and ignorant, I have always been secretly proud of my birthplace. Being born in a thunderstorm on a mountain in Indian country puts me ahead of Davy Crockett and in the same league as Moses and Quetzalcoatl. The circumstances call for something more than just a baby, I think. With a good public relations agent I could already be a legend—or even a myth—instead of an eccentric old professor from a place nobody ever heard of.

The land I want to tell you about—the land where I was born—is a small corner of Oklahoma lying north of the brown Arkansas River and east of the blue-green Illinois. For centuries it was avoided and bypassed, even by explorers, because the terrain was so rugged and the trees so thick that it could be crossed only on foot. It was shunned by the Indians themselves, except for small bands of hunter-gatherers, who left signs of their ancient campfires on smoke-blackened overhanging rocks near the springs. Some of their flint knives and projectile points can be traced back to a time before the Greeks had laid one stone on another.

The few old long-rifle woodsmen who wandered into the region later, in historical times, had to struggle through a maze of steeply forested cliffs and hollows where they seldom saw the sky and where the streams flowed every which way. Thus the land acquired the reputation of being not worth a white man's trouble, so it was given to the Cherokees along with a treaty and the customary promises of sovereignty.

By the time I was born, the Cherokee Nation was among the things that have been. Although the Cherokees were still there and the land still theirs, they no longer held the land in common. They had been coerced into measuring it out in sections and acres, according to the white man's idea of a homestead farm, with little regard for the suitability of the ground. In this way it had been apportioned to the people on the tribal roll, who for the most part received their allotments with mixed feelings.

It was not an easy land to live in. It had resisted human habitation from the first. It resisted clearing, it resisted cultivation, and it thwarted communication in every way. The often arctic winters were matched by summers of subtropical heat and humidity, when the unbroken forest bred an endless diversity of insects.

By 1929 only about 1 percent of the land had been cleared. The big game—deer, bears, wolves, and panthers—had been hunted out, but small game was as abundant as ever, and the streams were clear and clean and little fished. The Cherokees lived dispersed in their lonely cabins in the woods, accustomed to peace and poverty for two generations. The long blood feuds and factional strife that had mortally wounded the Nation were beginning to be forgotten, and violence was no longer an inevitable part of life. Fights and killings associated with drunkenness were common, but they were kept within predictable limits.

Coon Mountain got its name from the Cherokee family that was allotted a quarter of a section of land on the south end. Most of the Coon allotment was high bluff and rocky slopes, all thickly wooded. But there was some good ground up above the bluff that was level enough to farm, so the Coons cleared a small patch to grow corn and built themselves a log house with a fine sandstone chimney. My grandfather bought the place from Mr. Coon around 1916 and lived on it for some years before selling it to one of his cousins, from whom my father bought it in the late 1920s.

Coon Mountain was at the very center of the Cherokee country. I grew up there in the woods and rocky bluffs, as native to the ground as a persimmon sprout. Being as ignorant and happy as a child can legally be, I loved the country and thought it was beautiful. But like many love affairs, it was a one-sided relationship.

That land wanted no childish sentimental affection. So my love was always mixed with fear and the awareness that its peaceful beauty was haunted by an ancient deep-shaded anger that nobody talked about or seemed to understand. I knew its harshness from the first, and while I was still very young I found things to fear that were much more tangible than the ghosts of the old anger.

One summer morning I was playing beside my four-year-old brother in the shade at the back of our house, which had no underpinning but stood a foot off the ground there, supported on stacked rocks. We were just scratching in the dirt, in the way that only children find meaningful, when a big copperhead slipped out from under the house, taking a course that brought it within reach of my brother. He saw it, and having no experience with snakes, and hence no fear of them, he put his hand out toward it in a natural, thoughtless move. Then the copperhead struck faster than the eye could follow, sinking its fangs into the small web of flesh between his second and third fingers. It held on long enough to inject its venom, then glided swiftly away under the house.

My brother shrieked and began to cry. Fortunately Dad was close by—having come to the house from the field for something—and when he saw what had happened he did the only thing he knew to do, which was to cut across the fang marks with his knife so the bite would bleed freely. Mother brought a basin of kerosene in which she soaked my brother's hand and sucked on the fang marks to draw the venom. Then they put my brother in the car and took him to the doctor in town.

By the time they arrived, there was not much the doctor could do except reassure my mother that he believed the boy was out of danger. He warned her not to let him go to sleep soon, so she took him to her father's house in town and tried to make him drink black coffee the rest of the day. The snakebite and the accompanying shock and treatment were all painful, and he cried a lot, but in a few days he had recovered completely.

My memories of that traumatic day are vague. But a year or two later my brother and I had an adventure that I shall never forget. The events of that green summer morning are still vivid in my mind and will be with me forever.

We were on the narrow wagon road that went through the deep woods on the mountainside, on our way from our house to our mailbox, which was on the road that crossed the valley. We had passed a bend where the trail turned to follow the contour of the hillside for a hundred yards. At the end of that stretch the trail was closed by a wooden gate painted green, where the boundary fence crossed. We were about fifty yards from the green gate when a man came out of the woods beyond it. Surprised, we stopped and waited to see which way he went.

The man came up to the gate, apparently intent on crossing the wagon trail and going on up through the woods. By now we could see that he was nobody we knew, so we waited for him to pass on his way. We held back out of shyness rather than fear. We had not been taught to fear strangers. In those woods strangers never came, and we could have walked that trail a thousand times without meeting one. But we were shy, and the man was unknown to us, so we waited and watched as he approached the gate.

The gate was never locked, but it was easier to climb over than to open. As the man was climbing over it he looked up and saw us—and the scene became a nightmare. He stood up straight with his feet straddling the boards of the gate and raised a rifle over his head and flourished it as if to be sure we could see what it was. Then he put it to his shoulder and aimed it at us.

Half a second passed, then in a single unbroken sequence we gasped and turned and fled. We fled for our lives. Ever since that moment I have known the true meaning of *panic*. Spurred by terror and an awful awareness of the steepness of the trail and the shortness of my legs, I was possessed by a blind, mindless energy that sent me scrambling after my brother up the hard trail under the arching trees. We did not slow down when we got close to the house but threw open the yard gate and ran to where Mother and Dad were working in the backyard.

Breathless and sobbing we gasped out our story, our vision of evil at the green gate. Mother grew alarmed and angry and hardly knew what to do, but Dad's reaction was different. The sight of us and the state we were in had braced him for something dire and catastrophic. He expected to hear we had found the Meadows family all murdered on their front porch. So when he was able to get a clear idea of what had happened, it was a great relief to him. Nobody had shot at us? Nobody else had been shot at? To Dad, in effect, nothing had happened. He knew of course that putting us to flight had been somebody's idea of a practical joke. It could not have been planned in advance, it just happened. He'd never heard of boys being shot on their way to the mailbox. What made us think we were so special?

We learned later from Mrs. Meadows, who lived down by the mailboxes, that she'd seen a man headed up the mountain in the woods behind their house that morning. She'd recognized him as a man who lived two or three miles away, across the valley, and who was said to be not all there. He'd never been known to hurt anybody, so it is not likely that my brother and I were in any danger from him. But he scared the wits out of us, and it was a long time before his shadow was lifted from the green gate in the woods.

I had already had one close call with a gun when I was little more than a baby. One evening as I sat in my high chair at the kitchen table waiting for supper, Dad came in from squirrel hunting and leaned his .22 rifle against the wall just inside the kitchen door. My brother, for reasons nobody can remember, took up the rifle and pointed it at me and pulled the trigger. *Bang*! The .22 slug missed by head by a good six inches and buried itself in the door facing behind me. Not a bad shot for a four-year-old who could hardly lift the gun into firing position. I don't know what he had in mind—maybe he felt I had been getting uppity and needed to be put in my place. But a miss was as good as a mile, as far as I was concerned, and I never held it against him. The incident might have been soon forgotten had it not left a reminder—a little round hole in the wood of the door facing that grew more dim and indistinct every time we painted the woodwork but never disappeared entirely.

About this time, or perhaps a few months earlier, I was lying on a coonskin hearth rug in front of our fireplace while my mother swept the bark and wood trash into the coals under the burning logs. Unseen by her, a .22 rifle shell had got mixed in among the sweepings and was brushed into the fire. What happened next has two versions. The shell exploded, and I have always thought that the casing flew out and hit me above my left eye. But my mother says that she was the one it hit. She is the more reliable witness, but to support my version I have a scar in my left eyebrow. Whatever happened, I am sure there was enough of an uproar to satisfy everybody.

It was never my intention to write about all the times I have been shot at. As I was seldom hit, I will say no more of such matters. They were typical of the way of life where I grew up, and they show how things can get mixed together and mingled so they can't be separated—things like fear and beauty and love and danger.

Over the years I have developed a philosophy that I carry around with me like the spare tire in the trunk of my car, hoping I will not need it. In times of crisis, I tell myself that things can't be all that bad as long as nobody is shooting at me.

2 THE MANCATCHER ALLOTMENT

THE ROAD NORTH from our house was a wagon trail that struggled through a mile of woods to a clearing on the north end of the mountain. Red oak and hickory trees got in the way of the road and pushed it up over ledges and into swampy places as if trying to discourage it. The damp silt along the trail bore the tracks of deer and coons and sometimes the round paw-pad marks where a bobcat had put his feet down carefully in his own tracks, with his claws pulled up into his toes. In those high, remote woods the silence was profound.

The clearing where the trail ended was part of a forty-acre plot of land belonging to my grandfather. It was an unfrequented place, long abandoned when I first knew it and haunted by a silence deeper than the woods. On the north side of the clearing was a tall long-needle pine—the only tree of its kind on the mountain—that rose up over the hickories and oaks and marked the place where the old Mancatcher house had stood.

Back at the turn of the century, when the Cherokee Nation parceled out its land to the people on the tribal roll, the Mancatchers were allotted the north end of Coon Mountain. It may not have been the worst land in the nation, but it was not a promising place for a farm, being mostly rocks and woods and all but inaccessible. The Mancatchers cleared a few acres of level ground above the bluff and built a log house there.

They raised a little corn and tried to make a living on the place, but one winter at the time of year when the days are shortest they all got sick. Their closest neighbors lived more than a mile away, through the woods over the steep bluff trails, and the bad weather kept people at home. The Mancatchers were too sick to go for help, but nobody knew anything was wrong until some squirrel hunters stopped at their house one day and found them all dead. They had died of the measles, and they had been dead a week or more when their bodies were found. There were eight of them, including the children. Mancatchers.

Some relatives of the family buried them in the woods on the mountain, below the clearing, and after that they didn't like to go near the empty house. When a few months had passed they tried to sell that part of their land. But word of what had happened up there had gotten around, and it was easy to find people who would rather live someplace else. The house and field were abandoned for a few years, then the owners went to my grandfather, who lived on the south end of the mountain, and asked him to take the place off their hands at whatever price he thought was fair.

My grandfather hemmed and hawed. He already owned more land on the mountain than he needed, and the Mancatcher allotment didn't join his property. The only way to get to it was by going through the woods over the highest part of the mountain. The only water on it was a spring below the bluff. But in spite of all that he let himself be talked into paying two hundred dollars for the forty acres with the log house, which was a fair price at the time. He liked to oblige his neighbors when he could.

That fall he went out to look over the place, making a morning-long excursion of it with a wagon and team. He had to make up the road as he went, pushing a way through the woods and over limestone ledges. Even before he found the clearing he'd begun to suspect that the Mancatchers had put one over on him. For two hundred dollars he could have bought forty acres on the moon, where he could see it once in a while.

He found an eight- or ten-acre patch of rocky, rough-cleared ground where half-burnt snags and stumps rose out of thickets. The sumac and persimmon sprouts were higher than the sideboards of the wagon. He drove on across the clearing, crushing down sprouts and looking for something in the way of an asset. He headed for the tall pine tree at the edge of the woods, where the log house stood cold and abandoned, and reined to a stop in front of it. At close sight of the house, with its dark windows and gaping door, he changed his mind about going inside and stayed seated in the wagon. The autumn wind roared in the pine tree and the door of the empty house was swinging slowly in and out on its rotten leather hinges.

My grandfather didn't much care for the place. He took a long hard look at the swinging door, then he turned to look back over the neglected field, which didn't appear any better from this side than it had from the other. A heap of dead leaves that had collected in the lee of the steps rustled in a coil, with a low deadly sound, and a flock of crows jowered in the woods. He reached for the jug under the wagon seat, had a drink, and jammed the stopper back in, then he slapped the reins on the horses' necks and turned their heads toward home.

The next spring, he went back with three men to help him tear down the house and haul away the logs for some project of his own. He left the sandstone chimney upright, but without the house to support it the chimney soon fell and its stones scattered among the trees at the edge of the woods.

After that my grandfather hardly ever went near the place. It was so remote that he could forget about it most of the time— except when he got the yearly tax notice on it. He was a reasonable man about most things, but the sight of a tax notice brought out his worst side. He felt he was being imposed upon by having to pay taxes on the Mancatcher allotment. He would gripe about being taxed to death and having to be buried at public or tribal expense. Then, after paying the taxes of three or four dollars, he would talk of getting some of his money out of the place. One year he paid a man to go out there and cut sprouts and dig stumps, but before he could get it in shape it was too late to make a crop that year.

Taxes weren't the only problem. The mixed-up laws of the various levels of government made a good hunting ground for bush-league lawyers. A statute that was originally meant to keep the tribal land out of the grasp of unscrupulous buyers required the sale of allotment land to have the written consent of all potential heirs to the land. And so, whereas eight Mancatchers had died in sorrowful circumstances, others had lived and multiplied. Heirs to the Mancatcher place kept turning up from time to time, with claims to be settled at my grandfather's cost. His way of dealing with them was to offer to cancel the sale and accept a refund, which was the last thing they wanted. Then he would pay them something and get their mark or signature on paper. His record book has these entries from the early 1920s:

Smokey Mancatcher $15   (mark)
Dennis Mancatcher $10   (signature)
Cricket Mancatcher $20   (mark)
Pole Tie Mancatcher $15   (signature)

The amount seems to have depended on his mood. He was considered a rich man because he was one of the few around there who had any sort of cash income. He bore the obligations of his status with as much grace as he could, which is to say not much. He hated to feel that he was being taken advantage of. "I'll never see the last of them," he would say. "There's Mancatchers all over Wauhillau, clear to the river."

There was no point in his trying to sell the place. There had always been more land than money in the Indian nations. Besides, he would have been ashamed to offer it for sale. To do that, he would have to admit he owned it, which he could not bring himself to do. He always spoke of it as the Mancatchers' place.

The cause of all these small disturbances of my grandfather's peace of mind—the land itself—remained the abode of primeval silence, uninhabited and unseen, its existence unknown except to a few who would have preferred to forget it. Over the years, however, the stumps rotted away, the snags were pulled out—a few at a time, with horses and log chains—and even the sprouts were brought under control. A year came when my father, a full-time farmer from the age of fifteen, raised a corn crop on the Mancatcher field.

But the ground was poor, and two years of corn sapped its productivity for a decade. The only chance my grandfather ever had to put it to a good use came during the worst year of the Great Depression, when one of his grandnieces and her husband, Henry, turned up down-and-out, with two children and no place to live. He told them that if they were willing to live out there on what he called the lonesome forty acres, they could keep whatever they made on the place. Henry said he would be much obliged, and my father offered to help him build a place to live.

Henry's son, Floyd, who was in between my brother and me in age, soon became our closest companion. We walked out through the woods to watch the men building their cabin, which they put on the southwest side of the clearing, across the field from the big pine tree. Approaching the clearing, we heard the *chomp!* of axes biting chunks out of the trees and smelled the smoke of the brush fire and burning oak chips.

They cut and trimmed some big red oak trees and hauled the logs to a sawmill in Smith Hollow to get them ripped into planks.

Then they carried them back in the wagon—an eight-mile trip all told, over a road that served as a creek bed part of the way.

They framed the cabin of rough and unseasoned oak lumber and leveled it on flat rocks stacked under the base plate. They split shingles from oak blocks to roof it and finished it on the inside the best they could. It wasn't much of a house, but it smelled good. They built a kind of smokehouse next to it, but they didn't use boards for that. They built it the old-fashioned way, of smaller logs with overlapping notched ends, and roofed it with shingles like those on the cabin.

When it was ready, Henry took his wife and children and their belongings out through the woods in a borrowed wagon. They lived there four years, somehow.

If scenery was money, they would have been as rich as Republican senators. The site was hundreds of feet above the surrounding valleys. On the north side of the clearing, the woods concealed steep ravines and ledges that fell away to the creek five hundred feet below. East and west of the field, a narrow band of woods grew between the cleared ground and the edge of a sixty-foot bluff. From their cabin at the edge of the woods they could see through and between the trees into Echota Valley and twenty miles of wooded hills—blue lines growing fainter in the distance. The land down there had not been cleared, but you could see cabin smoke rising above the tops of the trees. And once in a while you would hear a dog barking, away off down in the hollows, but most of the time it was so quiet you could hear the trees grow.

They needed a well, among other things, but digging one meant digging through eighty feet of bluff rock with stone masons' tools, so they had to get water the same way the Mancatchers had, by carrying it in buckets from the spring five hundred yards away—first going down and then back up the dangerous bluff trail. This did not count as work, but as a chore for children to do. Floyd and his sister, Nioma, who was two years younger than he, carried water in buckets from the spring every day. They followed a dim, precipitous path that coiled around tree roots and corners of rock and slanted across a bulge on the face of the bluff. If they slipped they would fall into the jumble of rocks and vine-snared growth forty feet below.

My brother and I were mountain-born wood rats, and Floyd quickly took to our ways. We prowled the bluff and woods for chinkapins and blackhaws and winter grapes, and in the process we learned about the law of gravity. My brother survived three noteworthy falls without breaking any bones, but Floyd broke his arm and Dad took him to the doctor to get it set. It didn't do Floyd much good, however. With just one arm in a sling, he could still carry a bucket of water as well as he ever could. I profited from the example of my brother and Floyd and learned what risks were not worth taking.

We found the chimney stones and other signs of a house around the big pine tree. When we asked Dad about it, he said some people used to live there, but he didn't tell us about the Mancatchers and what had happened to them. So when we found the grave markers down in the woods we didn't know there was any connection with the place near Floyd's cabin. They were small slabs of marble, leaning or lying flat, with marks cut in them too dim and mossy for us to make out. Some had crosses chiseled into them to show they were the graves of Christians. We didn't know what a Christian was. Floyd had heard the word and thought he was one, but he wasn't sure. He had heard of Jesus and said that he had been born under an apple tree. My brother and I didn't know what we were.

There was a meetinghouse at Echota, in the woods west of the mountain, but it didn't have any kind of regular service then. It had a little wooden tower with a bell that was said to have been brought from Georgia over the Trail of Tears. It was rung only when somebody died, and the number of times it sounded told the age of the person who was dead. We used to hear the bell at Echota clearly on cold mornings in winter, but in the summer its tolling was muffled by the woods and sounded faint and far away.

In the fall we walked to Horn School in the valley with Floyd and Nioma. When the big school bell rang at four o'clock, we trudged homeward together along the narrow lane. Others left the schoolhouse with us but dropped off along the way. The bigger boys would talk in low tones about hearing panthers on the mountain and warn us to be careful going through the woods. My brother and I had only half a mile of panther-haunted woods to go through, with Floyd and Nioma for company. But once we reached our house, they were still a mile from home—a long mile of dim wagon road through the trees.

Sometimes we walked part of the way home with them, to encourage them. But we didn't like to go far. If we looked back after turning homeward, we would see them walking fast, or running, before the gray woods hid them from sight. They were hurrying to get home so they could take their buckets to the spring while there was still enough light to see the trail down the bluff.

One fall Henry and his wife got a little money ahead, and they bought a flashlight for Floyd and Nioma, so they could see their way on the trail after dark. They had never seen a flashlight and didn't know such a thing existed. It meant a lot to them, and they talked about it for days. They even brought it to school to show it off, and all the other kids were envious.

I didn't envy them on cold dark evenings in December, when the days were shortest. Or in the dead of winter when sleet storms left an inch-thick sheet of ice over the bulging bluff face. And I didn't envy them in spring when black storm clouds boiled up over the mountain and the air got green and as dark as night in the woods where they were going. I never envied them at all, at any time of year.

Toward the end of that decade, when the times got a little better, Henry and his family left the mountain and moved back into the real world. He and his wife worked in a defense plant and had what you could call a standard of living. They kept everything they'd made on the Mancatcher allotment in the years they lived out there. Whatever that may have been, it wasn't anything tangible.

After they left, the north end of the mountain was abandoned again. The squirrels and field mice moved in to ransack the cabin and smokehouse, and the sprouts started over in their relentless efforts to reclaim the field. But they had only a year or two to get established before my grandfather sold the place at last, cabin and all, for four hundred dollars. That was a fair price, I suppose, considering all the improvements he had made on it and the taxes he paid. In any case, his terms weren't hard—no money down and no interest on the balance, with payments due every year or so.

He told the new owner, Lester McLeod, that the title wasn't exactly clear. "You might not ever get it straightened out," he told him. "There's more Mancatchers than coppersnakes in this damned nation, and you'll never know when you get to the bottom."

Lester McLeod didn't care. He said he'd get along, one way or the other, and he supposed the Mancatchers could look out for themselves—or words to that effect.

I never met anybody who was well acquainted with Lester, so I never knew much about him, not even where he came from. We used to ask ourselves why a man with a family—or any man— would want to live on a place where he couldn't expect to hear half a dozen voices from one year to the next. We had a few theories about him, but they were all just speculation. We used to see him about once a month when he passed our house on his way down the mountain, going to town—a gray, whiskery man in overalls and straw hat, slouched over a team of mules, with his wife beside him on the wagon seat and two little kids peering over the sideboards. He always raised his arm in response to our greeting, but he never stopped to talk. He looked like somebody who belonged to a strict religious sect that refused to have anything to do with heathens. But Dad used to say that while old Lester might have his faults, he didn't have any more religion than a bobcat— and about the same kind. I don't know how fair that was.

Lester was a good bee hunter, and he used to sell a few buckets of wild honey. He probably had other skills too. But he wasn't any hand to read and write, as the expression went. I don't believe he bothered to put up a box on the mail route down in the valley. But he sent his children to school, after they were old enough to walk the two miles each way—or the mile and a half, if they took a short cut through the woods and down the bluff where there was no trail.

One cold winter night I was coon hunting with my uncle and another man when we came out of the woods into the clearing on the north end of the mountain, chilled to the bone. Seeing a yellow gleam in the window of Lester's cabin, we headed for it. The moon was full and bright, and the gray, still air was brittle cold. We stumbled across the rows of dry cornstalks to the cabin and stood out in front of it calling, "Hello!" until the door opened. Lester stood in the doorway outlined by lamplight as he tried to make out who we were.

My uncle said we wanted to get warm, and Lester told us to come on in. But before we could go inside there was a commotion as Lester's dog rushed out barking, and our dogs came roaring up in full force, and everybody was busy cussing dogs and kicking ribs until they could get acquainted and settle down.

We left the lantern on the ground and leaned our axe and rifle beside the door as we went in. Grateful to be out of the cold, we stood close to the wood-burning stove in the middle of the little room, and Lester grinned through his whiskers, showing his yellow, tobacco-stained teeth, as if he was glad to see us but didn't know what to do with so much company. When my uncle told him who we were, he seemed a little more at ease.

It was on a Christmas night, December 25. The cabin I had watched my father and Henry build looked much the same as it had years ago, when my brother and Floyd and I used to play there and in the woods. Lester had added a shed at the back for a kitchen, but there wasn't any room for furniture except beds and a stove. The stove gave plenty of heat for the small space. A kerosene lamp with a yellow butterfly flame burned on a wall shelf, its light dimly filling the room where we stood.

The door to the bedroom—the only cther room and hardly bigger than a closet—was partly open. Two small children who had been asleep there crept out and edged around behind us and climbed into the pile of old quilts on the bed behind Lester. They didn't say anything. Lester's wife must have been in the bed, but I don't remember seeing her and she didn't say anything.

Our faces were so cold-stiffened that for a minute we didn't try to talk. After we had thawed out, my uncle tried to make some conversation, but it was hard to know what to say to a man like Lester. When my uncle asked him if he'd had a merry Christmas, he looked puzzled and my uncle had to repeat his question. I thought maybe Lester was hard of hearing, but it seemed just as likely that he'd forgotten all about Christmas, or never even heard of it. There wasn't a sign of Christmas in the place—no tree or toys or presents, not even a cellophane candy wrapper. On the floor, near the chunks of firewood beside the stove, lay a brass cowbell with a leather strap and brass buckle, the only thing in sight that looked clean and bright, as if it were new.

Lester, standing next to me as the four of us hovered close to the stove, grinned sheepishly and looked down and seemed to think over what my uncle had said. He nudged the brass cowbell with his shoe. "Yeah," he said. "Christmas, all right." He paused and glanced around at us, and when nobody spoke he went on. "Christmas, all right. You know how kids are. Wanted me to get 'em something, you know. How they are, them kids. So . . . well, I had to get 'em a Christmas something. You know how they are . . ."

When we left the warmth of the cabin and struck out across the moonlit field, the air felt like you could have cut it up in chunks and carried it with ice tongs. It was one of the coldest nights I ever saw. I remember the gray moonlight on the dead cornstalks and the yellow gleam in the cabin window. I remember the look on Lester McLeod's face and the brass cowbell and the kids in the quilts.

The men who were with me that night do not remember those things. It may be that I remember the scene because I did not understand it. I thought Lester was being ornery and backwoodsy on purpose, and I was of the opinon that no man had a right to be so poor and ignorant that he could treat his kids like livestock.

But there is another way to look at it. Over the years I have given quite a bit of thought to that brass cowbell.

I went away not long after that, and it was a long time before I went back to the mountain. I never saw Lester again. Years later I saw his daughter—the little girl who had been in the cabin on that cold Christmas night—working in a diner in Stilwell. She was a pretty, bright-eyed girl of seventeen or so, with something about her that struck me as wild—in the animal sense of the word, not the usual human sense. The way she moved around in the crowded narrow space behind the counter made me think of a pet coon on a chain. Somebody told me her name was Mary Lou McLeod, but I didn't try to introduce myself. I would have had to ask her about her father, and I was afraid she might tell me that Lester had ended up in a nursing home somewhere, where they had air-conditioning and television and everything was real nice. And while I didn't wish Lester any harm, I didn't want to hear about that.

The north end of the mountain is part of my cousin's property now, which means that he pays the taxes on it. He says that for some reason the title still isn't clear. That doesn't surprise me at all. The title will never be clear, because the Mancatcher allotment belongs to God, if I may express it that way—and long before the Cherokees left the Smoky Mountains He put his mark on it and left it under a spell, so the developers would never find it.

Nobody has lived out there for years. The cabin is gone, and the weathered logs of the smokehouse are lying in the grass at the edge of the woods, a stone's throw from the bluff where the trail goes down to that spring. The big pine tree is gone, but a grove of seedling pines has sprung up there. The bright green of their needles contrasts strangely with the sky and the dark oak leaves.

The land will never recover completely from the shock of being cleared and plowed and planted in corn. But it is used only for pasture now, and the cows do well there. If you walk out into the clearing they will lift their heads and stare at you in amazement. They will come running to you from afar and follow you all around, as if they were hungry to know about the other world and longed to hear a human voice again.

None of the cows wears a bell around its neck. There is not much demand for cowbells these days. You need a bell when you have only one or two cows and turn them into the woods to eat what they can find. The bell can save you a lot of time and trouble searching for them in the woods. Few cows know when to come home.

Everything that I have told you about the place and the people who tried to live there is true. You can find the clearing on the Geological Survey map, if you know where to look, and if you should take a notion to go there sometime the cows will be glad to see you. On many days the only sound they hear is the wind or the crows, or the call of a dove like a muffled bell in the woods.

3 BLUE

DAD'S CAREER as a hunter began about the time he quit school, at the age of fourteen. He didn't just stop going to classes and drop out. That wouldn't have satisfied him. He liked to do a thing right the first time, so it wouldn't come loose and have to be done over. When he knew for sure that he couldn't benefit from any more formal instruction, he took the glass inkwell out of his back-row desk and stood up and hurled it at the teacher. It was a man teacher, of course; Dad knew better than to throw an inkwell at a woman. But for the rest of his life he regretted acting so hastily, becuase the inkwell flew wide of its mark and hit the blackboard. If he hadn't lost his temper he would never have missed an easy shot like that. He was so disgusted that he left the room without waiting to see what happened next.

After that he was free to pursue his own interests. He had no time for brooding over missed opportunities, because his family moved soon afterward to the Coons' old family allotment land, a long way from town, where they lived in a log house above the bluff, at the edge of the woods. His father had a job with the railroad and was gone from home much of the time. But there was no end of work to be done on the place where they lived, so Dad pulled stumps and burned brush and hauled rocks, trying to get the land that Mr. Coon had cleared in better shape to make a crop.

He was his own boss, and he took off to go fishing or hunting when he felt like it. He had a lever-action .22 rifle with a hexagonal barrel. Early in the morning he would go out to the edge of the bluff, sixty feet above the spring, and shoot at the squirrels in the tops of the oak trees. He took the squirrels home—those he killed—and skinned them and cleaned them so his mother could fry them for supper.

More than anything, he liked to hunt coons at night with his dogs. One of his uncles or cousins would usually go with him, but if nobody wanted to accompany him he would hunt by himself. The hills were as wild and rugged as at the dawn of creation, but the wolves and bears and mountain lions had been hunted out of the country and the coons and possums and other small game had multiplied. So his mother didn't worry about his being out in the woods till all hours on a cold night. He might fall off the bluff and break a leg, or his neck, but that was better than living in town, where there were always bootleggers lurking in the tie piles by the railroad tracks, gambling with cards, and all such as that. A boy couldn't get into much trouble hunting coons.

That was how he grew up, and he never got it out of his system. When he was grown and married and living on the mountain with a family of his own, conditions were still pretty much the same as they had been fifteen years earlier, so he soon got back in the habit of coon hunting. My brother and I were still too young to be his hunting companions, so he got one of his cousins, a boy of sixteen named Ralph Walker, to live with us. I have seen Ralph's initials along with Dad's in the concrete around the well head, with a date in 1930. That was the year when they started hunting regularly, two or three nights a week in the winters.

Dad had got a likely-looking pup that he set much store by, and he trained him to specialize in coons. He named him Blue, naturally, because he was what they called a blue-tick hound. Dad said that the name of Blue had something in it that made a hound feel important and respected and glad to be a dog. In any case he saw to it that Blue took himself seriously and didn't behave like a pot-licking rabbit dog, even when he was off duty.

Blue and I were about the same age, and Dad trained us both in the same way, using the same method. His system was simple and easy to grasp: if you did wrong, you got whipped hard enough to remember the occasion so you wouldn't repeat the offense. The fact that Dad gave Blue more of his time and attention than he gave me didn't mean he was partial to him. (If Dad was partial to anybody, it was to my older brother.) I didn't feel neglected, and I wasn't jealous of Blue. He didn't eat any better than the rest of us, and if he had to stay out of the house it was because of Mother's rule, not any unfairness on Dad's part.

I caught on quickly, and mostly I tried to do what was right in Dad's eyes, especially if he could see what I was doing or what I had done. Otherwise I used my own judgment. But Blue had too much integrity for his own good. He believed with all his heart that hens laid eggs for dogs to snack on between meals. Dad could think otherwise if he wanted to, but to Blue it was a self-evident fact. Because of this he suffered a lot of persecution. But he stopped short of martyrdom, and while he hated having to think, he must have thought it through and decided that no eggs and no whipping was better than both together. He must have sensed that Dad was being fair according to his own way of judging, for he didn't seem to bear any grudge against him.

Blue and Dad had too much in common not to be friends. Their passion for the woods and for hunting coons was a bond as strong as the ties of blood. With the wisdom of his species, Blue must have known that there were few men like Dad, who loved the dark beauty of the woods on a winter night and the thrilling joy of a scent trail. And he soon found that when they got down to the fine points, the nose-to-the-ground stuff that was the most important part of hunting, Dad wasn't as smart as he thought he was. It gave Blue plenty of chances to put Dad in his place.

They got all that settled in the first year, and in the next couple of winters Blue got so much practice that he became an expert on coons. In hunting season the coon population declined by four or five a week due to his efforts and the assistance of Dad and

Ralph. They brought in the coons they caught—returning long
after midnight, dead tired and half frozen—and the next day Dad
would skin them and stretch their hides on tapered boards. There
was always a row of coonskins hanging skin side out on the wall
of the old log house. He kept the skin of the biggest coon he ever
caught and tanned it soft, with all the fur on, for a hearth rug.
When I was very small, I could stretch out on my stomach on the
coonskin before the fire.

Once or twice a month Dad took the cured coonskins to town and
sold them for a couple of dollars apiece at the hardware store.
The storekeeper, whose name was Darby, was an amateur hunter
himself, and he was impressed by Dad's success, judging by the
number of skins he brought in to sell. Whenever he commented
on this, Dad always gave most of the credit to Blue, which was
only fair. Darby spread the word of Blue's prowess, and in a year
or two Blue had acquired something of a reputation and was a
valuable dog.

One day when Dad was selling his coonskins at the store,
Darby offered to buy Blue from him. Dad laughed and turned
down his offer, even after Darby raised his bid a few dollars. But
the next time he went in, Darby doubled his first offer, and the
long and the short of it was that he finally bought Blue from Dad
for twenty-five dollars. I don't think Dad wanted to sell Blue, and
in Dad's defense I should point out that this was in 1932, when
times were hard and nobody knew if they would get any better.
But on the other hand, he didn't really need that twenty-five dollars. He had worked in the Colombian oil fields for five years and
had saved enough money to buy the place on the mountain. He
was lucky enough to have a little money in the bank and be free
of debt. But a group of loafers was always hanging around in
Darby's store, and Dad could have got the idea that they would
laugh at him for a damn fool if he turned down that much cash for

a dog that hadn't cost him anything. Twenty-five dollars was more money than they saw in a year's time, all in one sum. To put the best face on it, Dad could have figured that if he refused, then Darby would raise his offer to fifty dollars—then he would have to accept it or feel like a damn fool himself. Whatever his reasoning was, it ended with his selling Blue down the river.

He came home and broke the news to us, and before we could grasp what was happening he hoisted Blue into the back seat of his 1929 Chevy and growled away down the mountain in low gear, heading back to town.

Mother was flabbergasted—although she may have been secretly delighted, since her relationship with Blue wasn't a meaningful one. Ralph was stunned speechless; and even if he hadn't been speechless, he was in no position to criticize Dad's judgment for doing anything that wasn't against the law. But for my four-year-old brother it was a different matter. He had always thought highly of Blue, and he didn't hesitate to criticize Dad if he thought he really deserved it. Dad and Blue were out of sight in the car when the enormity of it all registered on my brother's mind. I would call his response heroic. At first he wept loudly and bitterly, aware of his loss. Then as his sense of outraged betrayal got involved he raged and howled and bawled and screamed. He could have been heard half a mile away. He was absolutely magnificent in his refusal of all comfort. My mother and Ralph might have been able to calm him down, given enough time, but his shrieks touched a sympathetic nerve in me, and soon I was crying almost as loudly as he, and even more inconsolably for not knowing exactly why either of us was crying. Together we drowned the voices of reason and reassurance and drove Ralph and my mother to distraction.

Meanwhile, Dad was rattling along toward town with Blue in the back seat. I can't imagine what was going through their minds. The smoke from Dad's pipe, along with the jolting and swaying of the car, made Blue sick and he threw up all over the upholstery. Dad had to stop the car and roll down the windows and clean up the mess before he could go on. That may have helped to harden his heart, so he could say he was glad to see the last of Blue when he turned him over to Darby at the hardware store. Still, he can't have felt completely satisfied with the deal, driving home alone in the cold car, with Darby's twenty-five dollars in cash in his pocket. And what he found on his return was not the kind of thing to improve his mood.

My mother had needed all the help she could get from Ralph in her efforts to deal with two hysterical little boys, and Dad returned to find the house still in an uproar and supper not even in sight, much less on the table. The chores were still to be done, and Ralph was still occupied. So Dad took the milk bucket and stomped out to the barn. When the stock was fed and the cows milked, he joined the silent group around the supper table—silent, that is, except for an occasional spasmodic sob or hiccup. The yellow lamplight cast a dolorous gloom over the kitchen table, and nobody said anything more than "pass the potatoes." When he was through eating, Ralph pushed his chair back and went up to his quarters in the attic. Mother put the dishes into the pan and wiped the oilcloth-covered table, then she threw the remains of the biscuits and gravy out in the backyard, as always, before she remembered that Blue was no longer there to clean up the scraps.

My brother and I slid down from our chairs and went into the front room to sit side by side on the coonskin before the fire— silently wondering which one of us would be next to go.

Dad had got his feelings hurt, and he always refused to talk about it. I suppose I can't blame him, since he did not appear to much advantage any way you looked at it. But the story had to be told, of course, and after everybody had got over being sore about it we would tell the story of what happened to Blue every time we had company. People always seemed to enjoy it, and I guess that was worth whatever embarrassment it caused Dad.

Dad didn't enjoy having to think any more than Blue did. But he could think when he had to, just like a cat can swim when the occasion calls for it, and at some point during that wakelike supper it dawned on him that we live in an unreasonable world, and that there is no satisfaction in being able to hold your head up if nobody will look you in the eye.

When he had it figured out he got up and left the kitchen by way of the back door. We heard the car door slam a moment later, then the sound of him driving away, before the silence came flowing back into the house. A long time passed, and my brother and I fell asleep. I woke up when Ralph carried me out onto the porch, where we could hear the car growling up the mountain road. We followed my brother in the cold darkness down the steps and out along the flagstone walk as the headlights swung into view and the car rolled up to a stop outside the front gate. The windows of the car were down, despite the coldness of the night, and Blue was in the back seat with his head out the window. He was always a serious dog, not demonstrative. He stayed there with his head out the window, sniffing the mountain air for any trace of coons that might have moved in and tried to take over the place while he was away on business.

THE OLD HOME PLACE

MOTHER'S FAMILY was from Arkansas, and she liked to say that they came west in a covered wagon. But if you tried to get her to tell you about it she would laugh and admit that it was only a thirteen-mile trip and the wagon was covered because it was raining when they left Arkansas. So she didn't try to make much out of it except as a little private joke.

She was always proud of her Arkansas background. To her, Arkansas stood for respectability and cultural refinement, and anybody from an old Arkansas family was a member of the elite in her eyes, their social acceptability beyond question. She judged other states on their merits, except for Oklahoma, which was still Indian Territory and only pretended to be a state to please the federal government. She didn't expect much of people from Oklahoma. She sympathized with them and always treated them kindly, but she wasn't taken in by all that stuff about the so-called civilized tribes.

Her opinions were based on a fair amount of observation and experience, but mostly they reflected the views of her father, Monroe Garrison. He was one of the demigods of my childhood, but I will set aside affection and sentiment here and say that he had soaked up the conventional attitudes of his own time and was as prejudiced as a man with no cruelty in him can be. His prejudices were mostly theoretical, however, and by a quirk of natural justice any pain they caused was limited to members of his own large family.

Like most pioneers he was prejudiced against Indians, although he'd had almost no contact with them in Arkansas, and when he brought his nine daughters to Oklahoma he seems not to have thought of the possibility of an Indian son-in-law. He may not have known the extent to which the Cherokees had already intermarried with the whites. Few people in the Indian nations were without some degree of Indian blood, and under the circumstances family conflict was inevitable. First it was conflict between father and daughters, then between mother and father, and ultimately between daughter and daughter, and daughter-mother-father . . . The number and duration of these homemade domestic problems would have been almost worthy of King Lear. I have a feeling that Monroe Garrison paid the price, one way or another, for his human failings.

On dark winter evenings he would draw his armchair close to the fire and hold a long-handled corn popper over the flames, shaking it gently to keep the grains from scorching. Behind him the big, high-ceilinged room was in shadowy darkness, and the kind firelight showed his form somewhat shrunk with age and the effects of a severe illness in his thirties. His full hair was gray and close-cropped and his face as darkly weathered as an ancient mariner's from a lifetime in the out-of-doors. His brown eyes were alert and clear, and he smiled quickly, sometimes breaking out with an explosive roar of laughter that made people jump who weren't used to his manner. In his old age he had a potbelly, but his face was never fat, and his thin hands were always skillful at small tasks. When peeling an apple he would hold the blade steady with one hand and turn the apple deftly with the other, making a thin, unbroken strip of apple peel that descended to his feet.

He noticed things that others took for granted and liked to speculate on what he observed. He was an advocate of what everyone called progress then, and I never heard him sentimentalize the past. But it worried him to see the decline of the rural communities like those he had known in his youth. He correctly saw the automobile as the cause of their demise and felt that something irreplaceable had been lost. "People need to feel a part of something," he said, "that they belong somewhere." He refused to own an automobile himself until he was nearly seventy, but he learned to drive then, in a way, although he knew in his heart that the automobile was an enormous mistake.

He would have made a great lawyer, for he loved a lively discussion, and when he was intent upon being persuasive his voice was beautifully flexible. But his education had been limited to a couple of years in a country school in Tennessee, and though he could read the newspapers well enough, he preferred to have his daughters write his letters for him.

When he was ten, his family had left Tennessee and come to western Arkansas and acquired some good land southwest of Fayetteville. His father died of tuberculosis—contracted while serving in the Confederate army—and his mother died not long afterward. Monroe Garrison, who was a teenager then, left the family farm to his brothers and sisters and took up with a circuit-riding preacher named Cox—Andrew Youngblood Cox. I never knew what drew them together, but the youngster went to live with the Cox family at their place in the hills east of Evansville, a hamlet close to the border of the Cherokee Nation. That was in the 1880s.

The only photograph I have of A. Y.—or Andy Cox, as the old circuit rider was familiarly known—was made toward the end of his life. He is leaning on a cane, a small, dapper man with a gray beard. His eyes have the dreamy, impenetrable gaze of a fanatic, and he does not look very approachable. When I say he was dapper, I mean in the Arkansas sense: he is not clad in overalls or homemade shirt. Still, it is obvious that personal vanity was no part of his character. His clothes are a bit shabby, in fact, and do not fit him well. Only his bearing and stern eyes prevent him from appearing slovenly.

Circuit-riding preachers were not paid for their ministry. They were expected to provide for themselves, and they usually did so by farming. But clearing land and farming it is a full-time job, and often the families of circuit riders fared none too well. Only a number of sons willing to work hard could ensure the family's survival, and in that important matter A. Y. and his wife were blessed, with five sons and two daughters. As soon as the boys were old enough to split kindling A. Y. left more and more of the farm work to them and spent his time making his round through the hills on horseback. He knew the country for miles around and could always count on a meal or a bed for the night. After supper everybody would go down to the schoolhouse and A. Y. would conduct a service.

The people who came didn't always come to hear a sermon. The women and children and a few men would be inside the schoolhouse listening to the preacher, while the rest of the men and the older boys and girls stayed outside and got together. Circuit riders didn't minister to the genteel part of the population. To put it another way, the hill people of western Arkansas would have delighted Walt Whitman, but they would have sent Ralph Waldo Emerson into deep depression. There was as much good in them as there is in any class of people, I am sure, but they had been abused and mistreated and misunderstood and suffered from a kind of moral rust. Some of them, steeped in moonshine and biblical vices, were quite capable of biting the hand that fed them the spiritual bread. They did not bend their neck to every man that wanted to call himself preacher. And A. Y. Cox didn't look like much of anything—a seedy-looking, little old feller on a tired horse.

If A. Y. could stand up in front of those people and point out the error of their ways, there had to be some iron in him. And there was. You can see it in his picture. That dreamy, fanatical look in his eyes is like the smoke of a fire that could blaze out and send you reeling back. My uncle, who was no purveyor of idle or untrue tales, told me a story of the following incident involving A. Y. Cox.

It happened one night when A. Y. was preaching in a little one-room, out-of-the-way schoolhouse on the headwaters of Lee's Creek. The room was full, and people were hanging around outside in the dark, arguing and visiting, while the preaching and hymm singing went on and on. Those inside were beginning to feel the spirit, and A. Y. was hurling scripture and salvation in all directions. Just at the high point of his peroration, as he paused for breath and dramatic effect, an unidentified member yelled out a brief word of dissent. Maybe it was a challenge. Whatever it was, it was unseemly enough to stir A. Y.'s wrath and move him—for what I trust was adequate cause—to call down the wrath of God upon the one in that room who was closest to hell.

Just then, somebody with a gun in the darkness outside fired a shot through an open window and killed a man who had been listening to the sermon and minding his own business.

The shooting, it was learned, had arisen out of some local feud that in no way concerned A. Y. Cox. But it seemed so well timed to make some kind of moral point or other that people must have been uncertain whether to hang old Andy as an accomplice to murder or take off their hats to him as a man of God who practiced what he preached.

Fortunately, there was a side to him that was neither grim nor biblical. From all accounts he was a most gregarious man and seldom returned from one of his circuits without bringing somebody home with him for an extended visit. His wife never knew how many persons would turn up for supper or to spend a week under the Cox roof.

That was another burden to be borne by his wife, who had done most of the raising of their children. My own mother, who grew up in that household, used to say that her Grandmother Cox was a "Hughey" and that she had a reserved, English nature, cold at times. At bedtime she would urge visitors to feel at home and help themselves to the medicine cabinet. "There's all kinds there," she would say. "Take as much as you need." But I never understood if this was a sign of hypochondria or just her idea of hospitality—or both.

Sarah Jane—A. Y.'s wife—had two injunctions that she laid upon her numerous granddaughters. They were never to work for wages in another woman's kitchen, and they were never to marry a widower. The second holds a world of implications, inasmuch as A. Y.'s first wife had died after bearing four sons. But her granddaughters profited from the old lady's experience and heeded her advice, at least in regard to the two points she was so set upon.

Pictures of Sarah Jane show a grim little old lady in black, biting on the corncob pipe she smoked most of her life. She looks like Mammy Yokum in a bad mood. But I am sure the pictures do not do her justice. In any case, Mother was always very fond of her. I have sometimes thought, however, that Mother would have been very fond of Jabba the Hut, if he had grown up near the old home place in Arkansas.

The two youngest members of the Cox family were girls— Maude and Ruth. After the younger girl died at the age of five, A. Y. grew the more attached to his only surviving daughter, Maude. Accustomed as he may have been to the hard knocks of life, it came as a shocking blow when he returned from one of his excursions to find that the orphan boy he had taken into his home had eloped with his only daughter. Maude had run off and got married without so much as a blessing asked. "Why, I couldn't a been no more surprised," A. Y. declared later. "Than if hit'd been Sairy Jane!"

A. Y. was used to taking what the Lord dished out, and any hard feelings about the elopement were soon put behind him.

Maude and her husband lived on at the Cox place for years and thus took on the care of the aging preacher and his wife. That allowed the Coxes' sons to seek their own fortunes in their own way. It wasn't a matter of anyone usurping their place. A half-cleared, half-worn-out farm five miles east of nowhere, in Arkansas, was not the kind of estate families fall out over.

About this time, a railroad was built from Kansas City south to Port Arthur, Texas. It went along the east side of the Indian Territory, not twenty miles away, and it brought access to a wide market. The Coxes, who had been struggling for years under the cross of gold-based currency, found that they could make money at last—not just a dollar here and a dollar there, as they had in the past by peddling peaches or hauling a wagonload of apples to Van Buren over fifty miles of mountain roads, but money that made a difference, thousands of dollars in cash profits.

The source of these unheard-of riches? Pigs . . . in large numbers. The beauty of it was that you didn't have to feed them and worry about them or invest a lot of borrowed money in them. You took half a dozen pigs into the woods and turned them loose. Nature did the rest. Pigs are good foragers and know how to look out for themselves. They are immune to snakebites, and their natural enemies—bears and mountain lions—were no longer numerous enough to matter. The forest was mostly first-growth oak and hickory trees, which dropped acorns and nuts by the billions, covering the ground in fall with enough forage to last all winter. The pigs ate them with gusto and grew fat and sleek and multiplied apace. Last year's dozen pigs was this year's sixty or more. Two years later there were more pigs than you could count, pigs all over the place, thousands of them, rooting among the oak trees and ranging over the mountains in joyous abandon.

How these multitudes of independent, uncivilized pigs were coaxed out of the woods, lured from their mountain home, and delivered to the marketplace is beyond me. Anyone who has ever

tried to make a pig go where it does not want to go will understand the importance of that part of the business. Pig driving may
be a lost art, but the Coxes had mastered it. They were once paid
five thousand dollars in cash for a single herd of pigs. How many
such herds my grandfather and his brothers-in-law took to market
I don't know. They never became rich, but they were prosperous
by the standards of their community, and they used their money
in sensible ways. One became a leading dry-goods merchant, and
another went to Texas and raised cattle.

It was a good thing that they had got a little ahead, for the family was growing more numerous. The Garrisons' first child was a
boy, then six daughters were born at intervals of a year or two. By
the time he was thirty-five, Monroe was the father of seven. The
eighth child was another boy, then came another daughter, then a
third son. The last two children—to make a Victorian round
dozen—were both girls.

My grandfather would have been the first to agree that a man
with so many people depending on him should not get sick. But
in the prime of life he was stricken by a wasting illness that nobody could diagnose. When its progress was finally checked, he
could get about only with the help of a cane, slowly and la-
boriously. There was no place to turn for help in those days. The
stark and unlovely motto of Reconstruction days in the South
summed it all up: "Root, hog, or die!"

His wife could take him to the hot baths at Claremore. The
preacher could pray for him. His daughters could tend to him at
home. But none of them could do what his horse was able to do
for him, which was to enable him to carry on a man's part of the
world's work. He had always been a good horseman, but now his
horse became a necessary part of him. One of the children would
saddle his horse and bring it to the front porch, which was four
feet above the ground, where he could get into the saddle. And
once in the saddle he could make things happen.

He got a job as a rural mail carrier, riding his route on a big gray horse with official saddlebags, south from Evansville and over the mountain at a sedate pace, then down along the course of Mountain Fork Creek. For most of the year it was a healthy and pleasant occupation, amid beautiful scenery, and on cold days in winter it would have been a challenge that restored his health and confidence.

The visits from A. Y.'s cronies grew less frequent as the years went by, and the old circuit rider died before the end of the century. Left to his own choice, Monroe might have stayed in Arkansas, but his daughters were growing up, and the nearest school was five miles away. He bought them a carriage to drive to and from school, but the road down the hollow was mostly in a creek bed, and the creek could rise fast. The pig business was subject to the vagaries of the market. So when he found himself once more with some cash in hand, he took control of his own life for the first time. He bought some land near the little railroad town of Stilwell, over in the former Indian Territory, and built a big two-story frame house there. Then one rainy morning he loaded his family into a covered wagon and took them to their new home. In Stilwell he made his living as a horse trader and cattle dealer for some years and later went into apples in a serious way.

He always admired A. Y. Cox. Although he didn't seem to have been much taken by A. Y.'s preaching, he never failed to praise the old man's ability to spin a yarn. "When he told a story," my grandfather Garrison used to say, "he told it straight through, from first to last. He never had to go back and put in something he'd forgot, like most people do."

That is a knack I wish I had inherited from my circuit-riding ancestor, because I have left out many things about him and the old home place. With the reader's indulgence I will go back and put something in—just this once.

Not long after young Monroe Garrison went to live with the Coxes, somebody in the family got the idea of going west and taking a homestead in Oklahoma Territory. The opening of the unassigned lands—which resulted in the great land run of 1889—-was being talked up all over the country. Hundreds of thousands of acres out there, good prairie land, was just waiting to be claimed. You didn't even have to clear it. It sounded too good to be true.

So they outfitted themselves for a journey, with a wagon and plenty of supplies, and set out across the Indian Territory for the unassigned lands, 250 miles away. It was a trip of two or three weeks, over roads ranging from bad to terrible, in cloudy, wet weather, through unfriendly if not actually hostile country. My grandfather was a teenager when he made the trip, and it must have made an impression on him. But I never heard him talk about it. From what I can gather, by the time they reached their destination they had lost heart for the undertaking. They camped somewhere east of what is now Guthrie, and after looking around for a while they went back home without even trying to claim any land.

They didn't like the country out there, they said. The muddy creeks, the depthless red mud, the dust, the tangled growths of blackjack scrub oaks, the stormy skies, and the dirty tent settlements full of white trash and half-breeds. In short, they were homesick. Never until they went away had they fully appreciated the hills and woods and clear-water streams in the civilized land of Arkansas. Or felt the full strength of their ties to the old home place.

5 SPRING WATER

THERE WERE SIX springs on Coon Mountain that flowed all the year round, but every family that tried to live on the place had water problems. The trouble wasn't in the water itself, which seeped through eighty feet of limestone and was clear and cold and hard, but in the location of the springs. They were all at the same level, at the foot of the bluff, halfway up the mountainside, where the terrain was a chaotic jumble of fallen rock and big trees. The Coons, who were the first to settle there, had found the best spring and built their house as close to it as they could. But although the spring was only two hundred yards from the house as the crow flies, the trail over which they had to carry their water was more than twice that distance, a hundred feet of which was vertical. The trail can still be followed, and I have been over it many times.

The spring was in a cool, perpetually shaded place where white oaks and sycamores grew to great heights, their tops rising higher than the bluff. Here the face of the bluff had fallen away below the top rim, leaving a cavernous overhang where the spring made a pool among the boulders and trees. The streamlet flowed swiftly down the steep slopes, gurgling over rocks and under arched roots.

A few yards from the spring was a monumental fragment of bluff rock that had broken off eons ago and embedded itself in the ground. Its level top, twelve feet above the ground, had collected enough dust and debris to support small dogwood and blackhaw trees. Its sides were weather-rotted and honeycombed with fissures and had been the home of countless generations of mice and ground squirrels. A row of waist-high rocks nearby formed a natural enclosure around a small plot of level ground where arrowheads and other artifacts showed that people had camped by the big rock for thousands of years.

It was an ideal campsite for the old hunter-gatherers, there by the spring. But the spring was not convenient for a family living above the bluff. Five gallons of water is as much as a man can carry up a mountain. For the Coon family a trip to the spring meant half an hour's hard work. Carrying water day after day, year in and year out, would not get any easier as you grew older. No doubt this thought was on Mr. Coon's mind when he sold his allotment to my grandfather Ross.

Water problems were nothing new to my grandfather. He had grown up where carrying water was a part of the way of life. A fortunate few could build their house close to a spring. If so, they built a springhouse over the water and rejoiced. Those living on good creek-bottom land could dig a well and find water thirty feet below the surface. But most people lived on high ground, safe from floods but doomed to carry water all their lives.

My grandfather's family included three daughters and two sons, so there was a great demand for water for washing and cooking and other household uses. One of the boys could have been kept busy all the time carrying water, but my grandfather found a better way to keep them supplied. He cut a route to the spring, going through the woods from the wagon trail that went up through a draw on the south end of the mountain. The route he made was too rough and narrow for a wagon, but it was passable for a horse-drawn sledge. So he lashed some big wooden barrels to a sledge and was able to carry a hundred gallons of water at a time. The trip from the house to the spring was a mile when he went that way, and going to fill the barrels was half a day's work. But it provided water for a week's washing and cooking. For fresh drinking water he sent one of the boys to the spring every day.

When my grandfather sold the place to his cousin Dick Harris, he left the barrels for him to use. But Dick was a believer in progress, and he tackled the water problem head-on by digging a well—something everybody had said was impossible, because it meant digging through eighty feet of bluff rock.

How Dick got the job done I don't know. I suspect he must have hired a crew of professional well diggers, and that it cost him a pretty penny. But he got it dug somehow, and whoever dug that well must have remembered it for the rest of their lives. The well shaft was six feet across and about ninety feet deep. It was walled from top to bottom with unmortared stone and covered by a wood housing with pulley supports. It was a happy day for Dick and his family when they drew the first bucket of water from that well. They were free at last! Free from the iron bonds of drudgery.

The well was still in use when I was a child. Its water was drinkable, but there was always a faint mustiness about it that hinted of dead rodents. The well was so deep that when you raised the lid on the housing and looked down you couldn't see the bottom. If you dropped a pebble in it you could count to eight or ten before you heard a faint plot in the dark water far below.

When Dad bought the place from Dick Harris his first project—after building a storm cellar—was to solve the water problem once and for all. There was no plastic pipe or inexpensive kind of pump available then—and even if they had been available there was no electricity to operate them. Still, Dad was able to bring some new technology to bear, and what he had in mind was better than hauling a bucket of water on ninety feet of rope.

He had worked in the oil fields for ten years and learned something of the pipefitter's trade. He was able to perform the seemingly impossible feat of making water flow uphill. First he enlarged the pool where the spring welled up among the rocks at the foot of the bluff. Then he laid a two-inch pipe from the reservoir to a spot a hundred feet farther down the mountainside, where he he installed a ram pump—a device few people knew about then, or even now. I cannot explain how it worked, but the basic idea is that a column of water two inches in diameter can exert enough pressure to support a half-inch column many times its height. A stop-and-flow valve keeps the water in the smaller column from flowing back. Thus, with no external source of power, the ram pump pushed water from the spring to the house, a hundred feet higher. A half-inch pipe, suspended on wires, went up the bluff face to the barnyard, where it flowed into a thousand-gallon tank. From there it flowed by gravity to a tap in our kitchen. That was the extent of our plumbing, however. Dad didn't push his luck by trying to install a bathroom.

The pump produced only a trickle of water into the storage tank, but it worked constantly, and we were never short of water.

Dad was justifiably proud of getting the pump in place and working so well. He was very possessive about it, at first, and built a little housing for it of red bricks to protect its working parts. On top of the housing he mounted a heavy wooden lid with hinges and a padlock, so nobody would mess with it. That turned out to be a mistake, however. Within a week he found the lid of the pump housing pried off, its hinges broken loose. He muttered and cussed and mended the lid and locked it once more. Before long he found it broken open again. And again he fixed it and snapped on the lock.

At no time had the pump been damaged; there was almost nothing about it that could have been harmed—without taking a sledgehammer and blowtorch to it—so when he found the housing broken into for the third time he said the hell with it and didn't try to lock it up again.

He had no more trouble with it. The broken housing had not been the result of vandalism but of curiosity. People there spent a lot of time in the woods. The idea of private land wasn't very firmly fixed in their minds, and many could recall a time when nobody owned land personally. A piece of cleared ground was respected for whatever crops it might have, but the woods and streams were still common ground. There was no word for trespassing. People could go where they wanted to as long as they didn't bother people or leave a gate open.

So when they came across Dad's little brick box in the woods below the spring, they felt they had a right to know what was inside it. Well, maybe not exactly a right, but curiosity is no crime, and something in there was thumping away. When Dad left it open to view, they were satisfied, but to hear it in that box and not be able to see what it was—that was too much.

The ram pump worked for fifty years. Time and the weather demolished the wooden lid. The brick housing stood longer, but through the seasons of alternating frost and heat the mortar eroded away. One or two at a time, the bricks fell into the branch water and settled into mossy lumps. But even when there was no longer a brick to be seen that you could call a brick, the pump beat as steadily as ever.

It was not a perpetual motion machine. Dad replaced a bushing every decade or so, and at intervals of two or three days somebody had to go to the spring and take out a half-inch threaded plug at the base of the iron air chamber to drain the water out of it—an easy five-minute chore. On the coldest nights, when there was a chance that the water might not flow up the pipe fast enough to keep from freezing, somebody had to go down and open the valve to drain the pipe.

By the time my brother and I were old enough to do these chores, we knew the bluff trails as well as we knew our backyard. We found a place on the overhanging bluff top, sixty feet above the spring, where we could make our way to the spring by the most direct route. There was a corner of rock where you could find toeholds in the bluff and descend to a place under the overhang. Going back up was easy if you knew the technique. When

you came to the rock corner, there was only one way to place
your hands and feet. If you got them wrong, you were stuck until
you could figure out what to do. It wasn't hard. What took a bit
more nerve was going down the face of the bluff in the dark. You
had to go over the ledge backward, with your feet and legs dangling, until you felt the toeholds in the crevices.

It was a bit like rock climbing, perhaps. But to tell the truth I
have never had any stomach for that interesting but—to my
mind—risky sport.

6 FACES IN THE FIRELIGHT

COON MOUNTAIN was always a lonely place. I think that was one of the reasons we liked to live there. Lonely places make people seem important, if you follow me. But you couldn't live there all the time without feeling a touch of the blue lonesomeness that comes as a result of being cut off from the rest of the world.

I suppose lonesomeness is not a problem for anyone today, but back before there were telephones or radios it took a terrible toll in the backwoods homesteads and out on the empty plains. It was invidious and deadly, like typhoid germs in cold branch water.

The best defense against it was a large family. In our case, though our immediate family was small, we usually had a relative or two living with us on Coon Mountain. Among them was Dad's cousin Ralph, who lived with us four or five years when my brother and I were small. Ralph and Dad were good friends, even though Ralph was still a teenager. When Ralph's father died he chose to live with us and not go back to school. He helped Dad with his work and went fishing and hunting with him.

Ralph enlisted in the peacetime army, as soon as he was old enough, and spent a hitch in the Phillipines. He reenlisted and went to Officers' Candidate School and eventually became a commissioned pilot in the Army Air Corps. He had returned to southeast Asia before the war with Japan and was flying transports over the Burma Hump to China when he was reported missing in 1942. Nothing more was ever heard of him.

Another of Dad's cousins had come to stay with us, after Ralph left, on a more-or-less permanent basis—a boy of fifteen named

Earl Stevens. I was very young, and in my memory these two older boys are merged in a single character in the background. They lived in the man's world of the fields and woods and creeks.

Most of the time Mother was the only woman on the place. She was a cheerful soul who never complained, but she had grown up in a never-lonely household with eight sisters and three brothers, and she loved company, especially women visitors. She was delighted when Dad and Earl brought Grandma Stevens out to the mountain from Stilwell one winter. To people of Grandma Stevens's generation a visit meant a stay of at least two weeks.

Grandma Stevens, who was Dad and Earl's grandmother, was the earliest born of all the people I remember. She had grown up before the country had heard of Abraham Lincoln. She was a girl when the famous Charles Dickens came to America and ventured as far west as the Mississippi before turning back with a deep loathing for the Jacksonian democracy of the frontier. I doubt if Grandma Stevens had heard of him at the time. Her family was homesteading in the area of Iowa. She was nobody's Grandma then, of course. And her name then was not Stevens but Smith—Nancy Smith. But that is a bit misleading, inasmuch as her father was a full-blood Sac or Fox whose name was unpronounceable and pagan sounding and who, on being baptized, took the disarmingly Christian name of Smith. Her mother was of Dutch stock. She married Cal Stevens in the 1850s and threw in her lot with his family. Their origins were French and German, I believe, but whatever they were they did not interest themselves in their past.

They caught the California fever that swept the country in the decade before the Civil War and twice joined wagon trains setting out from Missouri for the golden West. On both attempts they failed to reach their destination. Once they got as far as the Arizona Territory before being turned back by the army, which was unable to control the hostile tribes on the route ahead. On their second try they made it no farther than western Kansas, where they lost their wagon and outfit in a prairie fire.

Their hopes still set on California, they tried to make up their losses by farming in Kansas, only to lose their crops to the Mormon crickets, as they called the grasshoppers. So they withdrew to the hills of western Arkansas, where there was plenty of game in the woods and good timber for shelter and forage. They hoped to live off the land while they worked to get another westward stake, but that proved harder than it at first seemed. The Boston Mountains were a wilderness and a rich hunting ground haunted by bands of sore Osages who bitterly resented the encroachment of the whites and Cherokees. Their unpredictable and disturbing ways kept settlers on edge for years.

History seems to have had it in for Grandma Stevens's family. Before they could get away from Arkansas, the war between the states broke out, and even the remote solitudes of their mountains were invested with its misery. They endured that long, drawn-out ordeal with the patient courage of those who have no choice. The end of the conflict brought little relief, for the aftermath was as bad as the war. Western Arkansas became a haven for diehards and renegades and other human debris from the wreckage of the Confederacy. They stripped and plundered. Nobody could get ahead any more, and California remained only a golden dream.

Grandma Stevens survived all that and more and lived on into her nineties. It was toward the end of her very long life that she came to visit us on Coon Mountain. I can see her by firelight at bedtime, a small but sturdy figure in a long brown dress, standing on the hearth as she combs out her long gray hair and coils it in a bun at the back of her head. When the winter twilight deepened, she would step out onto the front porch and scan the valley and the woods all around, as if to make sure the coast was clear of wolves and Osages before she turned in. For some reason the memory of Grandma Stevens evokes in me, even now, a puzzling and groundless fear of bears.

Mother and Grandma Stevens got along well. They understood one another, and each approved of the other. Neither of them was given to sulking or complaining, or to looking for things to take offense at. I doubt if two women separated by two generations as they were could have had more in common. But in spite of all that Grandma's visit was cut short.

A few days after she arrived, a long spell of mild winter weather was broken as strange, lead-colored clouds moved in underneath a layer of high, feathery cirrus. The air grew still and very cold under the thickening overcast.

We had a plentiful supply of good firewood, and Grandma Stevens didn't mind the cold. She pulled her chair closer to the fire and drew a quilt around her shoulders and carried on in good spirits. Even when it got so cold that we closed off the bedrooms and moved the beds into the front room where we could all keep warm, Grandma accepted it all cheerfully in the line of duty.

Then one night three or four inches of snow fell, and the grim possibility of being snowbound made Grandma Stevens pause to reconsider. At the noon meal she announced to Dad that she wanted to go home. The road down the mountain was still passable, but it was narrow and steep and hazardous, and Dad prevailed upon her to wait until the next day, when he figured the snow would have melted some and there would be no risk of winding up at the bottom of a ravine.

That night it snowed more, and snow kept falling on into the next day. The road down the mountain, far from being safer, was hardly visible any more. It looked as if Grandma Stevens was snowbound, whether she liked it or not. But when she understood how matters were, she fussed and fidgeted and could not know peace. She must go home, she said, before it got worse. Mother laughed and tried to cheer her up and promised to take her home just as soon as the road was safe. But the more she tried to divert her, the more determined she became. She wavered briefly and supposed she could wait a day or two, but soon she changed her mind again and nothing would do but she must go home to-day. Now.

At noon, at the dinner table, Grandma Stevens reminded Dad of his promise of the day before and confirmed her wish to go home. Dad was taken aback. He explained that conditions had got worse, not better, and that they would have to wait until they could at least see the road before setting out.

Dad was no good at persuading people to do what was obvious and sensible. Common sense and logical reasoning were no match for iron-willed determination. Only a fresh outbreak of hostilities, or a prairie fire, could had spared Dad what lay ahead. When he saw that Grandma actually expected him to get her home that very day, he vowed to have a shot at it, come what may, though the chances of a catastrophe were about 90 percent.

After the noon meal, Dad smoked his pipe and pondered the problem in grim silence. Grandma Stevens bustled about, helping Mother clean up the kitchen and stopping every now and then to step out onto the screened back porch and look over the snowy landscape, where a few flakes were settling lazily onto the five or six inches of snow already on the ground.

To Dad it was clear that to start down the mountain in his car would be an open invitation to disaster. The road was hardly wider than the car itself, with a deep ravine on one side and a high bank on the other. The first quarter of a mile would have made a good toboggan run.

Dad left the house with Earl, telling Grandma he would be ready to go within the hour. He had come up with an idea that he hoped would keep the consequences of folly within bearable limits. What he had in mind was something more often used by ships than cars; it was what sailors call a drag anchor. He cut down a medium-small persimmon tree and after lopping off most of its branches rigged it onto the rear of the car in such a way that he would be pulling it lengthwise.

The two men came back into the house all cold and snowy and prepared to load Grandma Stevens in the car, which now sat out in front of the house idling and steaming, with the persimmon tree tied on behind. They crossed their wrists to make a seat for Grandma, and she sat between them with her quilt around her shoulders while they carried her out and put her safely aboard in the back seat. Cars in those days had no heaters or safety belts, but Grandma Stevens can hardly have minded—with ninety years of wars and bushwhackers, locusts and hostile Indians and prairie fires behind her.

Earl wanted to go with them, but Dad said no, somebody had to stay and do the chores in case he didn't return. There were lengthy good-byes between Mother and Grandma, and it seemed like we had small chance of ever seeing Grandma or Dad again— until they were dug out of a snowbank in the spring. We all watched anxiously as Dad put the Chevy sedan into low gear and muttered away. Traveling at the speed of a glacier, the car nosed over into the ravine and out of our sight. We could hear it for a minute or two, growling and groaning down the steep mountain-side, then there was only a long silence.

We went back into the house to wait for Dad's return. Hours passed, and the gray winter afternoon darkened toward night as Earl went out to the barn and milked the cows and did the other chores. While he was gone, Mother set about fixing supper. She was quieter than usual, preoccupied with her thoughts for Grandma's safety.

We were on the point of eating supper when we heard heavy footsteps on the front porch and a prolonged stamping of snowy shoes. Then Dad came in, cold but cheerful, and reported Grandma safe at her own home. It had not been easy. The persimmon-tree drag anchor had worked fine. At the bottom of the steepest part of the road, where the danger of capsizing seemed to be past, he had unhitched the tree and forged on through the unbroken snow, getting stuck any number of times in an extraordinary streak of bad luck and providential rescues. His return alone in the car had been trouble free until he got to the mountain, where he had been obliged to leave the car below and trudge the last lap on foot.

Grandma Stevens never came back to see us, and one summer morning Uncle James appeared outside our front gate on his horse, having ridden out from town to tell us that Grandma Stevens was dead. Hers was the first death of anyone I knew. I saw the casket with Grandma in it resting in the parlor of Aunt Dora Littlejohn's house. I wish I could say that the solemnity of the occasion made a profound impression on me. But I don't believe that it did.

Between Fort Smith and Fayetteville, Arkansas, where Highway 71 winds over the highest shoulder of the Boston Mountains, there is a small roadside museum dedicated to Albert Pike, who once taught school there. From the terrace of the museum, if you look toward the southwest at the farthest high ridges of the mountain, you may still see the cabin where Grandma Stevens and her family lived during the hard times after the war, when the bushwhackers stole every cow and pig on the place and stole the very potatoes out of the ground.

She was the only person I ever knew who had been born before the Civil War, and she died before I was old enough to have any understanding of such things. Some of my forebears took part in the war, but whatever adventures they may have had were not passed down. My mother's grandfather Garrison had been with the Confederate Army, shoeing horses for the cavalry. And her great-grandfather, A. Y. Cox's father, is said to have been with the army of the South, though in what capacity I do not know. On my father's side, the only Civil War veteran I ever heard of was Uncle Anse, who had fought on the Union side and had been taken prisoner and sent to Andersonville, Georgia. He had been a timber cutter in western Arkansas, and how he came to be in the Union army I never knew. The whole region, however, tended to be divided in its sympathies. In fact, people there mostly loathed the war and had little use for either side. They had never owned slaves, and their reason for coming to western Arkansas had been to escape the slave system on the one hand and the factory system on the other. The war did not spare them, however, and few escaped being involved.

Uncle Anse survived Andersonville and came home after the war to be known for the rest of his life by the shortened form of the dreaded prison's name—Anse.

The faces of the old-timers who endured the war and its aftermath bear the marks of hardship. They look like those who have passed through fire and eaten the bitter corn bread of defeat. But now I come to the memory of a man whose face is marked by genial smile lines. He comes from the 1870s and thus was spared much adversity. He had three older brothers to look after him and two younger sisters to look up to him, and perhaps that is why he always seems to be expecting something fortunate and pleasant to happen. His white handlebar mustaches curl up like extensions of his broad smile, and I think that when he was born he must have smiled at the world and been smiled at in return.

Such at least is my impression in memory of the figure I see seated at our kitchen table in our house on Coon Mountain— Uncle Erskine Cox. He is enjoying a late, leisurely breakfast while he chats with my mother. She had a lot of uncles, but I think Uncle Erskine was her favorite, and I know why. She always admired a well-dressed man, and Uncle Erskine is a model of genteel attire. Perhaps he had visited his brother's big dry-

goods store in Stilwell before he came and got himself newly outfitted in spotless gray trousers and long black shoes, narrow and
flexible, that lace up to his ankles on hooks. He has laid his coat
aside, revealing a white shirt with stripes and modest suspenders.
His shirt cuffs are held well up on his wrists by elegant black
sleeve garters above his elbows.

Sitting nearby with my chin barely reaching the table, I watch
in silent awe as Uncle Erskine accepts a fresh cup of coffee from
Mother. After putting in sugar, he lifts the cup and pours the coffee into his saucer, making a shallow brown pool that steams and
fills the kitchen with its aroma. He then lifts the saucer full to the
brim and balances it on his thumbs and forefingers, with his
elbows resting on the table. Holding the saucer steady, he puts his
lips to it and blows on the coffee to cool it, then tilts the saucer to
sip from the edge. Not a drop falls onto the blue-and-white
oilcloth covering the table.

He puts down the saucer and wipes his handlebar mustache
with the side of his hand in a way that a cat might envy for its
self-assurance and refinement of manner. Not all our kin were as
polite and well dressed as Uncle Erskine. I wish he had visited us
more often, because I could have learned much from him.

For all his charm, Uncle Erskine was not the kind of man who
makes history so much as the kind who enjoys it. But the next
figure that rises out of the past is a man who seems made of history itself. There is something strange and archaic about him, a
dim figure who appeared out of nowhere a hundred years ago.
Although he is still remembered and spoken of, I never heard
anyone speak his name. He was always simply the Old Peddler.
He may have been Ahasuerus himself, the wandering Jew of me-
dieval legend. For he was indeed a Jew and a man respected by
all who knew him. He was the prototype, the very essence of a
Jewish peddler, from his black coat and hat to his strapped ped-

dler's case of wares and his ability to find a welcoming door in an alien land.

He traveled the dim narrow roads through the hills and woods, afoot or in a one-horse buggy, making his slow way from clearing to clearing. He stopped at the most remote and lonely houses.

I have seen him in our house on Coon Mountain, in the front room, kneeling on the linoleum beside his case of peddler's treasures, open for my mother's delighted inspection. She remembered him from Arkansas, where he used to visit her mother's house once or twice a year. She was pleased to see him and never failed to buy something from his pack. All I remember of its contents are spools of thread and packets of needles and little scissors, though there must have been much else.

I saw him no more than two or three times, when I was quite a small child. Many years later, when I had forgotten him and would hardly have believed in his existence, I learned what had become of him.

You might well think that, in the case of such a man as the Old Peddler, the odds were that he simply dropped out of sight. He occupied so small a place in the lives and thoughts of those who knew him that if he failed to appear he might not be missed for a long time. Then somebody would get to wondering about him and ask, "Have you seen the Old Peddler lately?" And speculation and rumor might have it that the Old Peddler was dead. Ignorance and suspicion would lead to tales of the Old Peddler's being murdered and robbed and his body buried in the woods in an unmarked grave. But as there was nobody who could report him as a missing person, there would be no investigation.

Such a fate could well have brought the Old Peddler's earthly journey to an end. Not a happy fate, certainly, nor one that he deserved, but a fate more plausible and likely than the actual events. For the fact is that the Old Peddler, far from perishing on

the lonely roads, had grown wealthy enough to retire with a fortune to his native land—wherever that was, somewhere in the
eastern Mediterranean world.

    But that is not all. Before he left the country, the Old Peddler
made one last trip over his lengthy route, making what was once
called a "sentimental journey"—that is, a journey to see old
friends and places for the last time. He had visited all his old pa-
trons, or their descendents, to thank them and bid them farewell
forever. This was told me by my Uncle James, who knew it to
be true.

The figure of the Old Peddler grows larger with the distance of
time, as do many of memory's people. Some of them take on a
grandeur and an aura of greatness that is no illusion. The seedling
becomes a majestic oak tree with the slow and incalculable effects of time, and the forces that might have destroyed a humble,
hard-bitten farmer may convert him instead into a landmark figure with the bearing and presence of a prophet.

Mr. Meadows was in his eighth decade when I saw him last, but
there was nothing of the frailty of the aged about him. He stood
under the elm trees that shaded his mailbox—in a spot where I
had spent hours as a boy, waiting for the mail—with his hands
folded over the end of a stout stick, leaning forward a bit to balance himself. His overalls sagged somewhat on his frame. His
hair was all white, and I was surprised to see that he had let it
grow uncut until it came almost to his shoulders. And even more
surprising to me, whose mental picture of him was twenty or
thirty years out of date, was his wide-brimmed black hat with a
flat crown. His appearance put me in awe of him until he spoke,
and in his robust greeting I recognized the familiar voice.

    I would never be a stranger to him. He called me by the name
that only my family knew and used, because he had known me all

my life. He had known my father all his life too. I have heard Dad
tell the story of how this man had bought him his first suit of town
clothes. They were kin, and they had been close in the old days.
But they had had a falling out and had not got along well for
years—an old story not worth the telling and not worthy of
either man.

The black hat looked good on him, with his white hair spreading below the brim. The man I remembered had been a poor,
work-worn, straw-hat farmer, ground down to a hard edge by the
mean conditions of America's lowest decade. Self-denial and
deprivation, I would have thought, should have made him con-
temptuous of all such fineries as black hats. But I had been
mistaken.

As a child I had always been a little afraid of him—as I was
afraid of all men at the time, sensing in them their pent-up rage
and restrained violence born of frustration with things as they
were, the awful labor year after year in drought and searing
heat, to raise a crop for which there would be as often as not no
market at all, at having to make things do more than they were
meant to do.

Hard times brought out the worst and the best in men. Families
with no income learned to subsist in the woods, like the families
who came to the same hills a thousand years ago, living on the
country. In spring they found where the mushrooms and wild
onions grew, and a dish of poke greens graced many a table. A
squirrel or two can be fried to feed eight, or boiled with flour
dumplings to satisfy any number, and hickory nuts stewed with
possum can be a tasty dish—unless you don't know where your
next meal is coming from, in which case it tastes bitter.

Many of us were driven to accept government help—government charity, we thought of it—from a government we despised,
as we despised all governments equally without discrimination.
Every week or two a commodity truck came by with grapefruit

and other staples for those who needed them. The grapefruit tasted bitter.

We greeted each other, after many years, and I felt honored by the warmth of recognition in his eyes. As we talked, he stood leaning on his stick and looking out over his valley land. The stick, unlike his hat, was old and worn. It had been cut from a locust sapling years ago. The bark had been peeled and the stubs of the lopped-off branches whittled smooth. Its wood was dark and shiny from long handling.

His children were all grown, of course, and the third generation was well into its own hardships and joys. He and his wife lived alone on the place now, renting out the fields for pasture and reserving a couple of acres for their garden. He had been a good farmer, and his patch of vegetables was a flourishing spot. Corns, beans, tomatoes, cucumbers, cabbage, potatoes—everything thrived in the enriched soil.

Before I left, he said, "Come on over here, I want to show you something."

He led the way to an old smokehouse that stood nearby. It had been refurbished and now served as a storehouse. He opened a padlock on the door and we went inside. When my eyes had adjusted to the dim light, I saw two big freezers along the wall, each five or six feet long. He raised one of the lids, and I saw the freezer was full to the top with frozen vegetables—okra, green beans, corn, peas—everything that could be kept by freezing was there. All of it was from his garden, of course. The other freezer was packed full of frozen meat—beef, pork, poultry. And this too had been raised on his place, though the cutting and packaging bore the marks of a commercial hand.

The two freezers held enough provisions for a full-scale Himalayan expedition. But the point he had wanted to make was clear. When the seven lean years returned, they were not going to find him unprepared.

THUNDER AT NIGHT

DAD TOOK an adversarial view of the weather in general and had a healthy fear of storms. When he moved his family to Coon Mountain he lost no time in digging a shelter in the hillside behind our house. We called it a cellar and used it to store food in—such things as eggs and cream and potatoes and home-canned fruit and vegetables—but when Dad built it he was thinking of a place of refuge. Its walls and arched roof were reinforced concrete, and the whole thing was banked and covered with dirt and sodded with thick Bermuda grass. It was close to the house; a gap of no more than four feet separated the cellar door from the door of our screened-in back porch. If we were blown off the mountain by a storm, Dad didn't want to hear anybody saying it was his fault for living in such an exposed location.

My first memories are of waking up on a stormy night as I was being carried to the cellar. These moments were stamped deep in my mind by the lightning and crashing thunder that always accompanied them. Still half asleep, I could smell the damp rough cloth of Dad's bathrobe and dimly grasp what was happening. Then came a cold blast of wet wind and the noise of gushing water as Dad hurried through the gap between the back porch and the cellar door with me in his arms.

With the heavy door shut and latched behind us, we descended the steep flight of concrete steps into the side of the mountain, leaving the storm outside. The sound of rainwater pounding on the house and pouring off the eaves came through the two narrow slits of windows high on the cellar walls, and flits of hail struck with metallic force on the iron cover of the ventilator pipe. But the elemental powers of the storm—thunderbolts sizzling to a crack of doom that shook the foundations of the hills—were held at bay, and I would fall asleep again and wake up briefly as I was carried back to my bed.

Dad's fear of storms was not unrealistic. Living on the mountain exposed us to a lot of weather, and we had more intimate relations with storms than most people do. They seemed so *close* to us, up there. And the clouds had more depth, a kind of extra dimension that made you feel you could reach out and touch them. The towering cumulus clouds that blacked out the sun and the slate-colored banks that rose out of the west at dusk could make me feel like the end of time was upon us.

In spite of the awe the storms inspired in me, I was not much afraid of them. I let Dad do the worrying about the weather. And while I found enough things to fear, I accepted the wind and rain and lighting as part of the territory.

When the prolonged drought of the 1930s was over, the weather grew stormier than ever. The spring storms of 1942 began with a tornado that brought death and destruction to Pryor, a small town sixty miles away. The monsoon-like system that spawned that deadly twister also brought great floods. Bridges washed out and dams overflowed and broke. I remember that on the eve of the storm the clouds had a darker and more threatening look than I had ever seen. Borne on a strong southeast wind, they tumbled along overhead, so low they caught on the hilltops and looked as if they could fall of their own weight. Before dark a torrential rain set in that lasted for hours, a sheeting deluge that curtained off the world and sent the creeks on a rampage.

Considering the devastation wrought by that storm, my reason for remembering it seems childishly inappropriate. Mother had planned an outdoor picnic dinner at our house that evening and invited her teacher friends from Stilwell. She broiled some chickens and made potato salad and I don't know what else, and as a special treat she had bought a little sackful of glazed dough-nuts from the newly opened bakery in town. But because of the storm nobody could get to our house, and we were stuck with all the food.

Mother was disappointed, of course, but the food did not go to waste. I took care of the doughnuts all by myself. They were the first doughnuts I had ever eaten, and once started on them I couldn't stop. They were light and fresh, with flakes of glazed sugar on the golden crusts—the kind that bakers keep under the counter and sell only to customers under twelve these days. I wish that my brother could have eaten some, but unfortunately he was cut off from home that night and I had to eat all of them. There couldn't have been more than a dozen, so I suffered no ill effects.

I felt bad the next day when I heard what the tornado had done to the people of Pryor. The storm that had caused their tragedy had brought me a windfall. But I was old enough to understand that it was better them than us, so I didn't lacerate my conscience about it.

In the summer of that year my cousin Cullen Bean came to stay with us for a while. I enjoyed his visits especially because, being a bit older than he, I could take the lead in whatever adventures and trouble we could manage to get into—stoning the wasps and smoking grapevine cigars until our tongues were so smoke-bitten we couldn't stand them. Once we found a little can of dynamite caps that Dad had hidden away back in a crevice in the bluff, pur-posefully aiming to keep them out of our hands. We didn't know what they were, and it was only because we were protected by the spirit of the mountain that we didn't lose any fingers before we took them to Dad and asked him what they could be. He took the box and a funny look came over his face and he started to say something. But he just muttered and walked off, shaking his head.

Cullen and I decided to camp out in the woods down by the spring, a quarter of a mile from our house. I had put up a little homemade teepee there and dammed the branch to make a pool, where we spent a lot of time on hot days splashing in water so cold it made us gasp. We carried our blankets and hatchet and other gear down to the site and went back for a frying pan and some bacon and potatoes and bread and salt. We made three trips up and down the steep trail, and when we had it all in place it was time to set about the interesting business of cooking supper— interesting to us at least for the novelty of it. I had watched Mother fry potatoes and bacon often enough to take a shot at it myself. So we got a fire burning and peeled some potatoes and washed them in the stream.

Our camp was among the tall trees near the overhanging bluff, where it was always cool and shady. The sun went down in the middle of the afternoon there and twilight lingered for hours.

While we were intent upon the potatoes, the fire burned out, so we had to put them aside and attend to that. We made a bigger fire than we needed because it was a little gloomy there, with the deep green dusk of the woods growing darker and the screech owls quavering along the bluff. But soon the bacon was sizzling and popping in the skillet and we sliced in the potatoes in hungry anticipation.

The chiming of thousands of insects came from the shadowy woods surrounding us. I would not have been brave enough to spend the night alone there, but I was determined not to show any nervousness. "When we've eaten supper," I told Cullen, "we'll make a fire in the teepee and the smoke will keep out the bugs." I didn't say so, but I was hoping the teepee would keep out the scary feelings as well.

I had learned how to make the teepee in a book about wood-craft. Nobody around there had ever seen a teepee. Certainly the Cherokees had never lived in them. But I didn't think of the

Cherokees as Indians. Cullen was a Cherokee, but I didn't think of him or his father, Uncle Mack, as Indians, even though Cullen had been born on allotment land in one of the first houses built around there. His house was the kind described by Mark Twain, a double log cabin with a wide breezeway porch between the two big rooms and a fireplace at each end.

Cullen liked my teepee, and we kept up our spirits with the thought that it would hold off any terrors that lurked on the dark mountainside.

Cooking proved slow work with us, and the potatoes and bacon tortured us with their smell as they cooked. Suddenly Cullen stopped stirring the potatoes in the pan and looked up. "Did you hear something?" he asked.

Before I could answer, I heard a far-off whoop, and I knew who it was. Pretty soon I saw Dad striding along the trail beside the big rock. I knew something had got his wind up because he was walking fast. When he caught sight of our camp he stopped where he was and yelled at us across the branch, "Come on, boys! Let's go!"

When Dad gave an order like that, he expected prompt obedience and no questions. It was best to let him have his own way, and I usually did. But under the circumstances I thought he owed us an explanation. I tried to ask why, but he cut me off, and though I didn't understand the words, his tone of voice was peremptory.

I muttered to myself and took the frying pan off the fire and set it aside. Cullen was waiting for my lead. "Let's go see what Dad wants," I said. "We'll come right back."

We splashed through the branch water toward Dad, who didn't wait for us but turned and walked rapidly back along the crooked trail through the trees. I was so exasperated that I failed to notice how much darker the woods had got and how the tops of the tall trees were roaring in the wind that came over the bluff top.

Dad wouldn't slow down. When he came to the steepest part of the trail, where it went up the side of a ravine behind the barn, he leaped up from rock to rock while Cullen and I panted along after him, still wondering what all the fuss and hurry was about. When we came out of the woods above the bluff we saw it—a cloud of awesome darkness, dead ahead and almost upon us. We broke for the house and cellar, still a hundred yards away, and the full force of the storm struck us head on and turned us sideways, staggering until we could gauge the strength of the gale. It came from the northwest, over the high woods north of our house, with a ragged, roaring tumult of clouds. Rain rattled on the tin roofs of sheds and stung our faces, and the wind was turning the locust trees inside out. Dad reached the cellar door and held it open until we were all inside, then he shut it and latched it and we went down the concrete steps into the pool of yellow lamplight where Mother and Grandma and my brother were sitting on kitchen chairs and upturned washtubs, looking dry and comfortable.

They greeted us kindly. But in our family every little incident had to be evaluated, and the general opinion was that Cullen and I were a pair of idiots who didn't have enough sense to come in out of the rain. No doubt the storm had come up just to make that clear to us. It had been our own idea to camp down there, and we had done so against the advice of others and in the face of a fair amount of warning.

I didn't have the heart to argue, things being as they were. But I might have pointed out that we had been warned against snakes, not storms, and that this storm had sneaked up on us without so much as a rumble of thunder. I muttered to Cullen that we would have been just as well off in camp, in our teepee. What was the point of camping out if you were supposed to run home when it rained? Cullen said I was right, but he may have just been humoring me.

The storm was long and violent, with wagonloads of thunder

tumbling down the mountainside. The ravine north of our house was a raging torrent in the night. The next day, along toward noon, we made our way down to our campsite in the woods. The sky was still heavy with dark, ragged clouds, and a gusty wind shook the water out of the trees, splattering us with chilly drops. What we found at our camp was in keeping with the weather and the mood of the day. Our teepee had blown down and everything was a tangle of poles and debris brought by the water that had swept the site. We found the frying pan lodged under a log and pulled our watersoaked quilts and blankets out of the collapsed teepee. Of the food we had brought—the bacon and potatoes and bread—not a trace remained. What hadn't been washed away had been cleaned up by the birds and squirrels.

It was a disheartening experience. It didn't take a lot of brains to see that Cullen and I had been much better off at home last night than here in the woods. But I couldn't help wishing that we had been left to ride out the storm on our own. It would have given us something to brag about and remind each other of for the rest of our lives. But the weather remained stormy for the rest of Cullen's visit, and we never got our camp-out in the woods.

In August the storms slacked off some; one evening Mother and Grandma decided to walk down to Horn School, where two women missionaries from back East had lately been holding religious meetings. My brother and I went with them, although not voluntarily. We went because Dad refused to go, and it was felt that somebody ought to escort the women. Also I suspect that Mother and Grandma thought a dose of religion would be good for my brother and me. We were in danger of growing up on Coon Mountain with an underdeveloped sense of sin.

So when supper was over and the dishes washed, we set off down the steep road under the dark trees on the east side of the mountain, where the dusk of evening had already settled. On our way down, we had glimpses through the trees of the valley fields, still shining and brightly golden in the sun's last rays.

Walking past the Meadows house we kept a wary eye on Blackie and Brownie, the two zealous dogs that guarded not only their house but the approach to ours with a savage grimness and low-throated growls that demanded respect. Once safely past them, we came to the mail road that went across the valley, a narrow lane of dirt and gravel sunk between fencerows overgrown with blackberries and dusty bugle vines.

Halfway to the schoolhouse, Grandma stopped at a rise in the road and looked back toward home. From this vantage point, Coon Mountain rose massively across the western sky. The sun had shut off its light abruptly, and rising over the mountain was the edge of a cloud that looked like it was made of coal slurry. A ribbon of brightness along its rim glowed with the light of the sunken sun.

We stood in the road while the two women asked each other if they should go home. Neither Mother nor Grandma wanted to be the first to call retreat, knowing it might be taken as a sign of wishy-washy faith. So we turned our backs on the ominous cloud and walked on down the dusty lane, where the tracks of the mailman's car were the only evidence of traffic. A quarter of a mile farther along, the road turned sharply to the right down a curve into the narrow vale where it crossed Horn Branch. The ford at the branch was only a few yards wide, but the water could rise suddenly after a heavy rain and for hours it would be impassable. The branch had its source at our spring on Coon Mountain, but before it reached the crossing it was fed by three other springs, the best flow of water being from the springhouse on the Horn place near the ford.

The Horn allotment had included much of the good valley land. Their big white house, shaded by elm and walnut trees, stood above the road. Walking home from school, we used to see

Mr. Horn sitting on his front porch, with his hands folded over a walking stick. He was a figure of great dignity in his black suit and white shirt, his gray hair showing under a broad-brimmed black hat. We thought he must have come from Georgia over the Trail of Tears. And he may have done so, though he would have been an infant at the time of that epic journey. His family was prominent and well educated. One of Mother's sisters had married into the family, and she and her husband had been teachers at the school in the early years of their marriage.

There was no one on the porch of the big house that evening as we walked down the curving road to the branch. My brother and I helped the women across the stream on teetery rocks. We trudged up a steep slope, at the top of which we left the road and crossed a stile, taking a short cut through the woods. The trail went through a wooded glen, passing the house where Mr. Kelley, the teacher, lived, then led up to a grove that bordered the school ground.

I was familiar with Horn School from the years I had gone there. It was built like every other country school in the state, I suppose—a white, wooden-frame building with a double-door entrance on one side, over which was a square bell tower. The playground was gravel and dirt, now overgrown with weeds and grass at the end of summer. The surrounding woods—off limits during school days—were bounded by an Abe Lincoln-type rail fence. On the north side, the school ground was shaded by tall hickory and elm trees, and a ravine served as a kind of moat between the school and the two large outdoor toilets.

Before going into the schoolhouse, Mother and Grandma stopped to scan the western sky again. The black cloud had advanced some, but there was no lightning or mutter of thunder from it. The landscape was steeped in a dusky green light, and the air was still and warm.

My brother and I took turns at the iron handle of the pump that stood on a concrete slab near the door. When the water was flowing, we drank from our hands and splashed it cold on our faces. While we were doing this a few other people came up—all of them women or children and all on foot.

We went in through the double doors into the small foyer, which even in summer smelled faintly of sausage and biscuits and molasses, from lunch buckets left in the cubicles during the school year. The bell rope came through a hole in the ceiling and was belayed to a cleat high on the wall, out of reach of the tallest boys. During school terms the big iron bell rang at five minutes to nine, to spur on laggards, and again at twelve o'clock, one o'clock, and four o'clock, to mark the progress of the school day.

We took seats once more in the double desks bolted to the floor in rows. In the center of the room was an empty place where a sheet of tin was nailed to the floor, for the wood-burning stove in winter. The teacher's desk was on an elevated platform at one end of the room, with a blackboard behind it. Tall windows in the north wall provided the only light and ventilation; the windows were screened with heavy mesh wire to keep out the insects and small animals.

During the missionary meeting—lamplit by yellow kerosene flame and made doleful to the point of tears by the strains of a portable organ—we sang "Beulah Land" and "Bringing in the Sheaves" and other old hymns. I did not know they were old, however, having never heard them before. Then one of the missionary ladies talked for a long time in a low and deadly serious tone of voice. About God, partly, but mostly about sin and repentance and being saved. The more I listened the lower and more miserable I felt. Outside the windows a breathless darkness had fallen and whippoorwills were calling in the woods along the branch. The insects had raised their chorus, and as the missionary lady talked on and on, her voice merged with the chirring of nightjars and katydids until the night was full of a mindless chiming. I felt like I was coming down with chicken pox.

Then came a low rumble of thunder that rattled the windows, and a damp gust signed in the trees and blew in through the wire mesh screens. As we stood to sing the final hymn, a loud thunderclap jarred the stovepipe dangling on wires from the ceiling and made the lamp flame waver smokily. We sang "When the Roll Is Called up Yonder," and Grandma glanced nervously at the windows, where green flashes showed a tumult of roaring leaves.

When the last words of benediction were spoken we went out into the darkness. By now I felt like a zombie on the night of the living dead. The sky was a continual shiver of heat lightning as the storm gathered inexorably. People spoke in low voices, asking one another what could be holding back the storm, and ran for home.

As I have said, Dad was firm in his refusal to attend these meetings. That took some strength of character, since it meant resisting the combined forces of his wife, his mother, and presumably God. But he was not one to remain comfortably at home when his family was abroad on a stormy night. When our eyes had adjusted to the darkness we saw him in the car at the edge of the schoolyard, smoking and fidgeting and calling to us to get a move on.

We were only a mile and a half from home, by road, but the condition of the road was such that the drive took fifteen minutes. The storm held off until we were growling up the mountain road in low gear. We were sheltered from its full force until we stopped in front of our house above the bluff. As we ran up the flagstone walk, the locust trees were bending to the storm and showing the pale undersides of their leaves. Inside the dark house, Dad found the flashlight and led us through the pitch-dark rooms to the safety of the cellar.

Somebody put a match to a lamp wick, and as the light steadied and grew, we found places to sit and catch our breath. By slow degrees we regained some of the composure and cheerfulness that had been wrung out of us by the storm—and in my case by an overdose of religion.

I'm sure that Mother and Grandma gave thanks to God for delivering us from the tempest's fury, but I don't remember any praying. Perhaps out of respect for Dad's feelings, and in recognition of his part in God's rescue operation, their prayers were silent ones.

8 A KITE TALE

COON MOUNTAIN was a good place to do almost anything that didn't require electricity or indoor plumbing—kite flying, for example. The field on the south end of Coon Mountain could have served as the site for an Olympic kite-flying contest, if such a thing had existed.

Kites were not common where we lived. I don't think anybody around there had ever seen a kite. Some of them may have known what a kite was, but most were as ignorant as my brother and me. Dad, however, had a somewhat wider background of experience because his father had worked for the railroad and moved around a lot. He showed us how to make a kite out of sticks and string and newspaper and flour paste.

We made a messy job of it and had no great hopes for our kite, because we had learned that things hardly ever did what they were supposed to do—that is, what we wanted them to do. We finished the project in order to please Dad, and when our kite actually stayed aloft on the wind, as a kite should, we felt a delight that was out of proportion to its performance. Some of our faith in things was restored, and we began to generate something like enthusiasm.

We begged for more string and kept splicing our line until we had accumulated so much that Dad made a reel out of a short board and some pieces of broomstick. It would take in two feet of line at each turn.

Our homemade kite flew well enough for a season, but when the next spring came we hankered for one of the store-bought kites we saw in town. Dad had grown up believing it was immoral to spend more than twenty cents for anything that couldn't be eaten or worn or planted, but a kite proved to be within his limits, and we eventually got one of the kind we wanted. It was white with red trim. We also got another two hundred feet of string to splice onto the string on our reel. Altogether we must have had a thousand feet of string, and our enthusiasm was close to becoming an obsession.

One morning we set out to make kite-flying history. It was a perfect spring day, with a steady breeze from the southwest. Our new kite was lighter than our homemade model, so we tied on a long tail of rags to steady it and took it up to the crest of the field on Coon Mountain, where there was nothing but sky in all directions.

The kite took to the air so eagerly that it snatched its tail out of my grasp and rose with a quick fluttering of its thin paper as fast as my brother could reel out its tethering string. He let it climb at a steady rate, testing the kite's action and finding it flawless. It seemed to give little shivers of pleasure every so often as it surged upward in the sunlight, as if pleading for more freedom. Higher and higher it rose. The sound of its fluttering came faintly to our ears. When all the string on our reel was at least unwound, the kite was a tiny dark shape in the sky, so far above us that we could no longer hear it fluttering. It swayed with a serene stateliness, tugging hard on the reel in my brother's grasp.

We anchored the reel under a heavy flat rock and weighted it down with more rocks until we were satisfied it was secure. Then we sat down to watch. We speculated on the possibility of getting more string somehow. "If we had enough string," my brother said. "You wouldn't be able to see it at all."

The kite had been steady at a forty-five degree angle, halfway between the horizon and the zenith, and swaying with a slow, consistent rhythm that shook its long tail out in graceful waves. The taut string arched upward from the reel in a pure white curve and faded into blue space so that the kite seemed unconnected to it.

As the spring sun rose higher in the sky, the day grew warmer and the breeze freshened to a wind. The kite continued to respond beautifully. The stronger the wind, the higher it soared. From its angle halfway up the sky, it surged steadily until it was two-thirds of the way up, pulling hard on the tethering line tied to the reel and anchored with rocks. In its struggles to go still higher, it suddenly gave a great lurch, then recovered, shaking its head. Then it began to put its head over at a perilous angle, first on one side and then on the other. In its present position its tail streamed out behind it almost horizontally, which lessened the stabilizing effect. It began to swoop and dodge about now, in a drunken way that boded no good.

"Got to bring it down," my brother said. "It needs more tail."

With considerable effort, we heaved the flat rock aside and, taking great care not to let the reel get out of his hands, my brother began to wind in the string. It was hard work. He had to dig his heels into the ground and lean back against the forceful pull from the thin white arc of string.

He had taken in no more than fifty feet when he fell backward onto the ground, still clutching the reel. The taut white arc of a line lost its shape and began to settle in slack loops from a point far up out of sight where it had broken.

My eyes had been on the kite. All at once it looked mortally stricken, like a bird shot in flight, and it lurched back and drooped and began to settle earthward, wagging hopelessly as the weight of its tail pulled it down and kept it upright as it quickly lost altitude.

We watched it fall, dismayed, knowing it would end up in the woods somewhere. If it came down around the bluff, we could have a lot of trouble getting it dislodged, provided we could find it and get near it. Then, as we watched it, trying to judge its distance, it dawned on us that the kite wasn't just falling, it was being blown away. The wind was going to carry it clear off the mountain to God knows where. We wouldn't even see it when it came to earth.

We scrambled to our feet and took off at once. Across the field and past the house we ran, then down the ravine on the narrow road winding down the mountain. We plunged full tilt and headlong into the tunnel-like steepest part under the trees. We had now lost sight of our kite.

As we were pounding past the Meadows house, tennis shoes slapping the dusty gravel, Robert Meadows caught sight of us and ran out in our wake, unable to imagine what could have sent us racing down the mountain in such uncontrollable haste. We gasped a hurried explanation, without slowing down. By now we had caught sight of our kite again. It was still fifty feet above the ground, descending slowly on its tail in an old field a couple of hundred yards away.

There was less wind there in the lee of the mountain, and the kite touched down close to the spot where we had spied it. Robert caught up with us and went along as we climbed over the mass of bugle vines on the fencerow and into a field of weeds and persimmon sprouts and a few dried cornstalks from last year's failed crop.

We picked up our kite, looked it over, and found it little the worse for its fall. The excitement of the chase was over and now we faced the tiresome chore of recovering our string—hundreds of feet of it strewn over fields and woods. We knew from experience that it would be caught on everything—tree limbs, barbed wire, weeds—and have to be retrieved piecemeal. Robert offered to help us, and we began to backtrack on the line of kite string, winding it on a stick as we went.

The field where our kite had fallen was part of the Feathers place. The older members of the family didn't speak much English, but there was a boy about my age living there whose name was Billy. Robert knew him better than we did.

They lived in an old gray house at the edge of the woods, at the foot of the mountain. While we were getting our string untangled from the cornstalks and barbed wire, Billy Feathers came out of the house and walked toward us—a barefoot, black-haired kid in faded blue overalls. He was a shy boy, even shyer than me and much shyer than Robert. He stopped a little way off and watched us.

Robert greeted him, and Billy mumbled something in turn. He kept his eyes on the kite. Robert said, "Ever see one of those things, Billy?"

Billy Feathers shook his head and looked baffled. He stared at the kite as if it had a strange power of its own. Robert told him what it was, but the word didn't mean anything to Billy.

A mischievous gleam came into Robert's eye. He winked at us and said to the sober-faced boy, "What did you think it was, Billy? When you saw it come down out of the sky?" He was teasing him now.

Billy looked back at the spot where the kite had fallen and said softly, "I thought it was a ghost."

⑨ BALING WIRE AND BINDER TWINE

WHEN IT CAME to machinery Dad was conservative. His common sense told him to make the most of it, but his instincts warned him not to get involved with it. He'd had some success when he installed the ram pump at the spring below the bluff, but that had been due to his knowledge of pipe-fitting and concrete mixing rather than mechanical aptitude on his part. And while the pump worked for fifty years, he never understood exactly *how* it worked. I don't think he wanted to know how it worked. He had nothing of the mechanic in him, and the less he had to do with the mysteries of physics, the better.

He always owned a car and was careful to fulfill his obligations to it and make the ritual sacrifices ordered by the high priests at General Motors. He would change a tire if he had to, or patch an inner tube. But if the car wouldn't work, he would no more have tried to fix it than he would have tried to operate on a sick horse. He even paid his friend Jim at the station in town to change the oil, because doing that himself would have put him into the kind of intimate relationship with the car that he was determined to avoid. He had bought it not because he liked cars but because he liked to fish, and with a car he could go down to the creek in the middle of the afternoon and get back home in time to do the chores.

Conservative as he was, he was less so than most of his neighbors. He owned more farm machinery than most, including a mower, a hay rake, a corn planter, a baler, and a binder. All these contraptions had come with the place when he bought it, so he didn't feel responsible for them. They were so old that no speck of paint remained on them; the iron of which they were made was a uniform rusty brown. They all worked on the simplest of mechanical principles and depended on horses for their operating power.

The idea that machines are labor-saving devices has been widely accepted, and I suppose there is enough truth in it to be misleading. It is in large part a myth contrived by people who want to sell machines rather than use them. If we examine the matter we will find that only some machines save labor. Others do the opposite—they create it. For example, cutting and storing hay in a barn is a simple if laborious job for a man, a boy, and a horse-drawn wagon. But baling the hay after it is in the barn calls for a piece of heavy machinery, a boy, a horse, and the labor of five men. The old-fashioned hay baler created more labor in its day than any invention since the plow.

Dad's baler was used by the farmers living nearby in the valley, and in return for using it they helped Dad bale his own hay. The baler was a ponderous and heavy machine, awkward to move. Horses pulling it up the mountain road had to get down on their knees and struggle. When they got it up on the mountain, the men would set it up close to the big double doors at the front of the barn. It was mounted on flat-rimmed iron wheels six inches wide and had a long wooden tongue on the front, to which the horses were hitched when moving it. Its middle section was a ten-foot iron chute through which the hay moved as it was being pressed into bales. At the rear was a big, wide-mouthed iron hopper that stood high off the ground, with a wooden platform bolted to one side.

When the baler was in operation it tended to enslave everybody within reach. It may have been old-fashioned, but not in a traditional farming way. It was more like a factory line. Let me explain how it worked.

Two men with pitchforks carried the hay out of the barn and

heaved it up into the hopper, where a third man stood on the wooden platform to push it down into the depths of the baler with a pitchfork. The rate at which they worked was set by the machine, and they had to match their pace to it.

Two more men, one on either side of the iron chute, worked at the wiring. Here each man's movements had to match those of his partner on the other side, step for step. Long pieces of new baling wire, precut to the proper length and with a loop at one end, lay close at hand within reach. As the hay moved through the chute, which was partly open along the sides, one man pushed the end of a new wire through one of the grooves in the wooden spacer block between the bales. Then he took the end of the wire that the other man had poked through from the other side and bent it around to insert it through a groove in the next spacer block. Here the end of his own wire would have been pushed back through another groove, and by threading it through the eyeloop in its other end he could draw it tight with pliers and twist it so it wouldn't come loose. These two wires held the bale together lengthwise. Two more were then put crosswise around the bale, which would come out the end of the chute a little later.

It was a tiresome and repetitious job, in which every movement had to be done in accordance with the machinery, with no margin for individual variation when it came to taking a break or stopping to blow your nose. If you lost the rhythm or kinked a wire, the whole operation had to stop while you got straightened out. The men who did the wiring had the most demanding job, but they had the advantage of being able to work seated on bales of hay.

The pressure needed to squeeze the hay tight in the bales was supplied by the horse, whose work was as tedious and repetitious as everybody else's. He was hitched to a long bar that turned like the long hand of a clock around a pivot at the end of the baler tongue, where a gearbox converted horsepower into mechanical force through a complicated linkage of gears and levers. The horse had to walk at a steady pace in a circle, the monotony of his task broken only by the need to lift his feet when he stepped over the baler tongue once on each round. He soon wore a dusty path in his route. After a week of baling, the barnyard would have a worn circle, like a druid ring, that would remain visible for half a year.

It was part of the boy's job to keep the horse reminded of his duty. He also carried the spacer blocks that came through the chute back to the man on the platform hopper, who inserted them at intervals into the maw of the baler. Moreover, he was expected to keep the baler crew supplied with buckets of fresh drinking water and a handy dipper.

A new generation of machines has long since replaced the kind of baler I used to watch in operation. You can see them as you drive along the interstates in summer—dinosaur-size monsters that traverse the prairies, leaving rolled bales as big as buffaloes in their wake.

Nobody has ever raised a voice to lament the passing of the old-fashioned balers, and I will not be the first. The amount of labor they created was prodigious, and essentially a waste of time. Baled hay is no better than loose hay. Cows do not care if hay is baled or not. It was baled in order to have a standard measure by which it could be sold. When it was fed to livestock, the wires holding the bale together were cut and discarded. But that seemingly worthless by-product of baling made the greatest contribution to Western civilization. Sooner or later the discarded strands of baling wire would be retrieved and straightened and used in one of the makeshift repair jobs that were always confronting the farmer. A list of the uses to which baling wire has been put would be endless. What couldn't be fixed with baling wire often didn't get fixed at all.

The only thing that rivaled baling wire as an all-purpose fixer was binder twine—the by-product of yet another obsolete machine, the binder. This turn-of-the-century marvel was the most compli-cated and clattery product of Yankee ingenuity I ever saw. Drawn by two horses, it could cut wheat or oats and tie the grain in sheaves, which it left on the ground in its wake.

A binder had more moving parts than a steam engine, and every part in it was connected to everything else. It was fascinat-ing to watch. The sickle-bar blades went snicker-snack, back and forth, under a big wooden reel with slats that knocked the cut grain back onto a canvas conveyer belt that took it up inside the housing, where levers and rods and plungers were going in every direction and the binder twine unwound from its big spool inside an iron canister.

Any machine that can do all that and tie knots at the same time deserves respect, and it is apt to have quirks of its own. Our binder did not like rough ground. (No machine does, of course.) And since rough ground was all we had, the binder often refused to work.

One of Dad's friends, a fellow with a bit of the tinker in him, liked the binder and could coax it into working as long as half an hour at a time before breaking down. But Dad had no sympathy for it. He expected it to do its share of work like everybody else, and when it wouldn't work he got mad at it. He would come stomping over to the binder and look at it like it had just run over his coon dog. He would shake his head and take a deep breath and turn away, and you could see how badly he wanted to take a crowbar to that machine and show it who was boss.

The binder responded to him as you might expect, so he always let somebody else drive it, sitting up on the high iron seat over-looking all those clackety moving parts, while he worked along behind with the shocking crew, helping to stack the sheaves prop-erly so they wouldn't be ruined if it rained before we got them in the barn.

One summer morning after the sun had dried the heavy dew, Dad and three other men started cutting the field of wheat north of our house—eight or ten acres of rough ground that would take all day to cut, if they had good luck with the binder. We boys were in the field to watch and run errands. Mostly we chased the rabbits that got caught in the standing wheat as the binder made its first swath around the edge of the field. We followed the shocking crew across the widening strip of stubble ground. The field of standing grain diminished slowly, and as the sun grew hotter the rabbits began to panic and bolt for the woods at the edge of the field. We gave chase and sometimes managed to lay a hand on a young one.

Dad was not wont to mix work and play, but any kind of hunting always appealed to him more than any kind of farming. In an unguarded moment he let himself get caught up in the spirit of the chase. As he was working along stacking the wheat sheaves, he glimpsed a streak of gray fur racing through the stubble on a collision course with him. When it scampered by his feet his hair-trigger reflexes clicked; his hand shot down and he nabbed it with a sure, strong grip and clutched it tight—but not for long. What he had grabbed was not a baby rabbit but a big mama rat, who lost no time in letting him know of his mistake by biting clear through the fleshy part of his hand, between his thumb and forefinger.

Dad yelped in shock and surprise, flinging his arm up and sending the rat sailing through the air in a furry arc to land in the woods, where she was out of play.

The binder crew knocked off work to rest in the shade awhile, and Dad went to the house to attend to his injury. We went along with him to watch, but we kept quiet. He poured a basin full of kerosene and soaked his hand in it, letting the wound bleed freely. The blood did not mix with the kerosene but settled in dark, oily globules in the bottom of the pan. When the bleeding stopped, he wiped his hand clean and tied up the bitten place with a clean rag, pulling the knot tight with his teeth. Then he went back to join the men waiting at the edge of the field and fired up his pipe for a smoke before going back to work. He warned us to keep our mind on what we were doing and to be careful grabbing at rabbits.

There was no way he could blame that mishap on the binder, but I know he didn't regard as pure coincidence the fact that it had happened while they were cutting wheat with that clattery piece of junk, because not long after that, he traded off the binder for four half-grown pigs. He wasn't a sharp trader usually, but on that deal he obviously came out ahead.

The only time Dad broke his rule against complicating his life with more machinery, he lived to regret it. He was taken in by an ad in the Montgomery Ward catalog for a machine that he thought would give him more time to fish and hunt. It was a mill for grinding stock food. Doing that job at home would save him making trips to the feed mill in Arkansas—all-day expeditions and costly to boot. The mill in the catalog had no engine, but that was all to the good. He wanted no part of anything with rings and cylinders and wires and plugs and all that stuff. This was a belt-driven mill, designed to run off the power of a car engine. This meant it had to be hooked up to the car, of course, but he had learned to live with the car on his own terms and for that reason he let down his guard.

The catalog description said anybody could operate the feed-grinder. The instructions that came with it were clear and simple. All you had to do was to bolt the mill in place and position your car—a 1929 Chevy, in this case—so that its left rear wheel was in line with the drive wheel of the feed grinder. Then you jacked up the rear of the car until both rear wheels were off the ground, and blocked the front wheels fore and aft. The next step was to remove the left rear wheel and install the drive belt on the machine and over the bare hub of the wheel. The drive belt was a twenty-foot piece of heavy, rubberized canvas six inches wide. If there was too much slack in the belt, you could install an idler pulley, for which there were separate instructions. The final step was to start the car engine, shift to low gear, and let the engine idle while you fed your grain into the hopper and collected the ground feed in sacks.

The instructions didn't say what to do if the belt wouldn't reach from the mill to the hub. The procedure in that case was painfully obvious: remove belt, replace wheel, lower car, remove blocks, and back up the car a foot or two. Then jack up the rear end, remove left rear wheel, block front wheels, install drive belt, etc.

The catalog description made all that sound easy. But it was written in a kind of sneaky way that flattered the prospective buyer, implying that he was the kind of man for whom mere things would not dare cause any problems.

It wasn't a bad machine in some ways. It was made of heavy cast iron and would never wear out. Dad bolted it to the porch of the old house, and within a day or two he was grinding away like mad. But the trouble was that it took so long to get all those ducks in a row that he hardly broke even in time and money and endured a lot of nervous irritation in the bargain. Mostly the problem came from the drive belt, which had a maddening tendency to slither off the wheel at one end or the other.

He made the best of it, however. As soon as he realized that he had encumbered himself with another labor-making piece of machinery, he ignored it completely. He acted as if it was not there—which took some doing, considering that he had mounted it in such a conspicuous place.

The last time he tried to use it he found that the drive belt wouldn't fit the hub of his new car, and that gave him the excuse he had been looking for. One day when his friend Henry was there, Dad offered to give him the feed grinder.

Henry said he was much obliged, but since he didn't have a car or anything, he probably wouldn't get much good out of it. So they talked it over a while, then Henry helped Dad load the feed grinder on a wagon, and the two of them took it out and threw it over the bluff. It landed down among the jumble of rocks and trees and grape vines where nobody would ever see it. That may not be a good way to solve problems, and it was not usually Dad's way. But it was plenty good enough for the feed grinder.

10 SMALL WARS

WHEN GULLIVER WAS in the land of the giants he was attacked by a swarm of wasps as big as bluejays. He drew his sword and stood up to them like a man, he tells us, and killed two and drove the rest away. It is a good story, but we have only his word for it. It strikes me that Gulliver's wasps weren't made of the same stuff as the wasps we used to fight. Our wasps were made of poison and rusty steel, and if they had been as big as Gulliver's, half a dozen of them could have depopulated our school district. To have fought them with swords would have been idiotic. The only way to put one out of action was to disassemble him with a wrench and screwdriver.

Our wars with the wasps had no flash of gallantry. They were brutal, stone-age melees in which the object was to kill the enemy, destroy his home, and murder his offspring. They were wars of angry passion—on our side, at least. I don't know how the wasps felt about our army of three small boys—my brother, my cousin Floyd, and me—but in a fight they acted as if they were just as angry and determined as we were.

The war went on sporadically for three or four summers. Sometimes we would forget about it for weeks at a time, then one of the hot-tempered little beasts would sting somebody and bring calamity to his kin. The sting of a wasp is not soon forgotten; it hurts with the sharp, steady pain of a barbed insult and arouses vengeful feelings.

Or perhaps we would see that the wasps had had the gall to build a nest in the big persimmon tree across the road, in plain sight, as if to dare us to do anything about it.

We could mobilize for war in minutes, but we didn't rush into battle. Our fighting spirit was tempered by fear and the memory of pain and by the knowledge that the wasps were formidable enemies. If they had been equipped with a brain worthy of their physique, we would have had no chance against them. Clearly they weren't afraid of us. They didn't even respect us. And it was only because we were smarter than the wasps, ignorant and grubby and scared though we were, that we dared fight them. That is not a boast, just a fact. If the wasps had had any intelligence it would have been a different story.

The wasps, with their stubborn instincts, persisted in building nests where we could see them, usually on the limbs of trees, where they were vulnerable to our paleolithic tactics. A wasp nest as big around as a bucket makes a small target at fifty feet, but if you throw enough rocks you will score some hits.

The three of us would take up positions close to a tree or something else we could hide behind, then we would advance as close as we could and throw a volley of rocks. The wasps always counterattacked at once, whether we hit their nest or not. We retreated behind trees. The wasps may not have had much of a brain, but they could tell a boy from a rock. When their paper castle was jarred by one of our missiles, they never went for the rocks that were causing the destruction, but straight for the throwers. Fortunately, while they could tell the difference between a boy and a rock, they had trouble distinguishing boys from trees. If we stood unmoving, flattened against a tree, they could not find us unless one of them chanced to fly close enough to pick up the scent of fear.

It was a war with little glory and no heroes. After the initial assault we fired at will and tried to stay out of the line of fire from both sides. Sooner or later a rock would knock away part of the nest or put a hole through it. But we didn't stop until we had dislodged the remnants. Then we went home satisfied, while the wasps fell back to regroup, by no means defeated.

Such a war has no decisive battle or dramatic climax. The most memorable engagement occurred on one hot summer day when we found that the wasps had built a big nest under our very noses. That is, it was under the eaves of a shed close to the house. Its location could not have been better chosen, because it was impossible to hit with rocks and, being under dry shingles, could not be burned out.

Our initial assault, which was poorly planned, only aroused the wasps. They drove us to shelter inside the shed, where we waited for them to cool down. At this point, my brother's talent as a tactician served us well. As a rock thrower he was only a little above average, but when it came to finding a way to get things done he was head and shoulders above the rest of us, as the event showed.

On the inside wall of the shed was a rack where Dad kept his cane fishing poles. On a bench near the door were some burlap sacks, and back in a corner stood a big empty steel barrel with one end cut out of it. Floyd and I could have stayed in the shed all day without seeing the connection between those things, but my brother took it all in and saw what had to be done.

When the wasps had calmed down, we rolled the steel barrel out of the shed and slowly maneuvered it into position with the open end away from the wasp nest. The closed end of the barrel had a two-inch hole in the center where a nozzle had been attached when the barrel was used as a shower tank. My brother crawled into the barrel, and I followed him. We squirmed around to sit sideways, with our feet propped against the steel side, while Floyd put rocks under the barrel to keep it from rolling over. He handed us one of the cane poles, which my brother pushed through the opening at the end, letting its tip rest on the ground. When we were all set, Floyd hung a couple of burlap sacks over the open end of the barrel and retreated to a place of safety.

Up till now we had kept quiet and moved stealthily, trying not to disturb the wasps. But we could tell by the way they kept their wings cocked while working on their nest that they didn't trust that barrel a bit. Inside it we sweated and prepared to make our move. My brother raised the end of the pole toward the nest, getting leverage on the butt end that was inside. With the coolness of a future tank commander he kept his eye to one of the bolt holes as he slowly got the range on the nest.

The first swipe of the pole failed to dislodge the nest and infuriated the wasps anew. They fell from the nest and attacked the barrel in squadrons. We could hear them thump against the steel and zoom away to try it again. Others attacked the end of the pole, which was wavering in dangerous proximity, threatening their nest. The pole wobbled, then slashed at the nest and got some leverage on it. Before the wasps knew where all this was coming from, it was too late. Their nest was broken off at the stem and fell to the ground beside the shed.

We had to stay inside the barrel, quietly sweating in the almost unbearable heat, until the wasps could grasp the fact that there was nothing left for them to defend. Then we crawled out into the cooling breeze, unstung and elated, feeling we had raised the art of combat to a higher plane.

Twenty years later, in another country, I put my hand into a hedge I was trimming to take out a piece of trash that had lodged there. I felt a sudden stab of fiery pain, and before I could withdraw my hand there was another. And another! I retreated in haste and saw on my knuckles three rapidly swelling white spots, each with a pinpoint of red in its center. I could feel the wasp venom spreading up my arm, and with the rage of battle growing in me for the first time in years, I planned a one-man campaign.

No more childish rock throwing, no more games in barrels. Before the baking-soda poultice had dried on my hand, I went after the wasps with a kerosene-soaked rag tied to the end of a stick and did for them what Charlemagne did for the Saxons—that is, I made sure they would not cause any more trouble.

More years passed peacefully, and I no longer cared to study war. I grew serene and Wordsworthian. I began to see in nature a great and marvelously intricate web of life, in which all things had their necessary place. The wasp nest in the persimmon tree, had we but known it, meant fewer insects of even less favorable aspect.

Then one summer morning not long ago, as I was working in my backyard garden without a shirt, I slapped thoughtlessly at what felt like a fly on my back. Then something like a needle of red-hot steel struck me between the shoulder blades and burned like a flaming arrow. I turned in shock, just in time to see a flash of red-and-black wings fluttering upward through the sunny air.

At once the venom began to work its awful change in me. Kind old Doctor Jekyll, the benevolent ecologist, shriveled away in the throes of a wrenching transformation. His garden hoe fell at his feet. On the spot where he had been stood a mean, scowling little savage who shook his fist at the sky and muttered primitive curses, swearing eternal vengeance on all the tribes of Vespidae.

11 THE HILLS OF SUMMER

THE HILLS WERE alluring on a shimmery hot afternoon in August, promising relief from the steamy heat of open places where the sun beat with unrelenting force. In their green depths the cold branch water splashed over mossy rocks, and the glare and fever of noon never disturbed the peace of twilight. We felt that if we could escape into the depths of the woods we would come to a place where the sun was only a glimmer and the fiercest thunderstorms only a darkening tumult in the treetops.

But this was mostly a delusion, a dreamy fantasy born of our despair and desires. If we pushed our way through the green wall of foliage into the promised shade, we found the woods already occupied. And though the occupants were very small, they were also numerous.

Nature-photography artists, those who dwell so lovingly on the beauties of our insect friends, would have liked Coon Mountain in the summer. We had all the common bugs—spiders, flies, gnats, millipedes, mosquitoes, cicadas, katydids, grasshoppers, locusts, june bugs, ants, moths, and butterflies, to name but a few. We had those with stingers—wasps, yellow jackets, hornets, bees, scorpions, and such. Then we had some slightly exotic species like the praying mantis and devil's walkingstick. Some we didn't even have a name for. I suppose tarantulas ("translers," we called them) aren't insects, but whatever they are, we had them as well. Centipedes too.

Those with stingers were not the least of our worries, but they could at least be seen and avoided most of the time. That was not so in regard to ticks, which clung to our clothes and buried their heads in our skin before we knew they were there.

It was the tiniest insect of all that inflicted the most misery upon us. I speak of the chigger. This wretched mite is so small that only the keenest eyes can see it. The only chigger I ever saw looked like a mere pinpoint of red-orange pigment on the dark green surface of a persimmon leaf. I know it was a chigger because Grandma identified it and called it to my attention, and if anybody knew a chigger when they saw it, Grandma did. The chigger was so minute that, while I have very good eyesight, I couldn't make out any of its features.

Chiggers teemed in the underbrush and weedy grass, where they were easily brushed onto our clothes or skin. We wouldn't feel them until they had burrowed under our skin. After a while we would feel a slight itching at our wrists and ankles, or around our waistlines where our belts rubbed. We would scratch the itching places thoughtlessly and get a momentary relief. But soon the itch would return, worse than before. And the more we scratched, the worse the itching became. We could scratch until our skin was raw, but nothing could ease the burning discomfort. Our only remedy was kerosene, applied to our skin as a repellant before going into the woods, or put on afterward as a counterirritant to smother the embedded chiggers in an oily film.

I have heard of an oriental variety of chigger called paddylice, which carries typhus germs. Thank God we were spared such an affliction. If the chiggers we suffered from had carried a communicable disease, they would have made the country uninhabitable.

Living so close to all these insects, we had got used to them. They took over the woods for six months of the year, but even in midsummer we claimed the rights to the cool, shady places by the springs. As a rule, however, the woods in summer were not for the uninitiated, and there were places where even the initiated did not care to go—places where everything loathsome came into focus. I grew to know these spots and passed them, when I had to, with a prickly fear and dread. They were typically small openings in the woods, such as a break in the canopy left where an oak tree had fallen. In such places the sun struck with its steamiest rays.

One of these ill-favored spots lay at the foot of a ravine on the road up Coon Mountain. For the rest of its way the road was shaded by arching trees that let through only scattered, coin-sized drops of sunlight, and I would walk down the shady tunnel of the ravine in the cool morning air feeling healthy and cheerful. Then I would come to the open place, into the glare of the midmorning sun, and I would suddenly grow conscious of all the little things around me. Cobwebs would cling to my face and I would break out in a sweat, itching all over. From a crevice in the big rock beside the road a lizard would fix me with an unblinking stare. My eye would light on a six-inch centipede—a great orange-and-black crawler—writhing out of sight under a log. Or I would look up at the limb of a persimmon tree and catch sight of a grossly oversize waspnest crawling with big red wasps, their wings cocked for action. And the air would be heavy with the sickly sweet smell of vegetation.

As I walked through this open place, the cicadas and grasshoppers would stop their chant, leaving ominous silence. Then I would hear the far-off, hollow notes of a woodpecker drumming on a dead tree, tapping out a message to some awful force of nature that cared nothing for me or any of my kind. I often felt the approach of terror and had to make an effort not to break into a run. I knew that if I ran I would be overtaken by panic. I had to pass that way almost daily, and I could not afford to be afraid of things I couldn't see.

I don't mean to imply that there was anything mysterious or psychic about those places and their effect on me. I simply feel that some places are good and some places are not—judgment based on what I feel is good for *me,* of course. What is good for snakes and centipedes is another matter. It may be that the ecology of those wooded hills, the biome, which had stabilized so long ago, had no niche for man. When we settled there we tore the fabric of life, so that what we see now is the unraveling of nature. But I had better leave that to the ecologists to explain. Personally, I have grown more superstitious with age and now consider myself more of an animist than a scientist.

I have been speaking of the time when I was quite young. After my tenth birthday I was not afraid to go anywhere in the woods by myself. But at that age I wasn't interested in the woods for their own sake. I went into them shyly, looking for things I could use or eat, keeping an eye out for things that could hurt me. There was little of the hunter in me. If a bird or animal sat still long enough, I would shoot at it with an arrow or with my BB gun. Once I came face-to-face with five young owls perched side by side on a low-hanging branch. They stared at me in astonishment as I sneaked away and hurried back to the place where I had left my bow and arrows, running all the way. But when I returned the owls had wisely left their perch and I could find no trace of them. They had not been in much danger from me, however, as the only thing I ever killed with an arrow was a chicken—a pointless act of vandalism that I later had cause to regret. If I had been a born naturalist I would have kept still and watched those owls instead of running for a weapon. I might have learned something. But I had somehow got the idea that knowledge—of the kind that mattered—was found only in books and in older people. It never occurred to me that I might learn anything worthwhile by looking closely at things.

North of our house the domed summit of Coon Mountain rose three hundred feet higher. This high ground, being too steep and rocky for farming, had not been cleared. Ledges of gray lime-stone were exposed, and the soil was thin. But elms and oak and hickory and hackberry trees grew there, and it was a good place to find blackhaws and redhaws in the fall.

At the south end of these woods were ledges where you could look down over our fields and see nothing else but the hills and sky beyond. The hills reached to the horizon, fold on fold, their bluishgreen tint growing lighter with distance until they merged with the sky.

Near this picturesque site (where my mother always dreamed of building a house some day) and a little way back into the woods, was a place where the lichen-covered limestone of an an-cient seabed was laid bare. Thorny bushes and low trees took root in the cracks, but nothing else could grow there. In the center of the stone-floored clearing was a water hole—not a mere puddle or mud hole, but a stone-sided miniature lake ten feet across and a couple of feet deep.

There was always water in this pool, although it had no inlet or outlet at the surface. The water seeped into it from the thick layer of porous stone that lay under the high ground to the north. A few centuries ago, or perhaps even more recently, the pool had been a spring from which water flowed the year round. The course of its former stream was now a gully that went down the mountain in the ravine near our house. At one time it had been a beautiful mountain stream, with so full a flow of water that it had eroded away a great chunk of the bluff and mountainside.

But over the centuries, as the summit of the mountain itself wore away, the water-bearing strata diminished until they could not absorb enough rainfall to feed the spring all year round. It flowed intermittently then, in rainy seasons, until it was no longer a spring but only a mysterious pool in the rocks amid the woods. Bands of prehistoric hunters had camped on the site many times. We could always find arrowheads around and below the place.

Near this pool I saw the only flying squirrel I ever saw on the mountain. My brother and Robert Meadows and I were in the woods when we saw something scamper up a nearby tree. We threw sticks at it until it suddenly leaped from a high branch with all four legs widespread at its sides and glided to the foot of another tree fifty feet away. It ran up that tree and soon made itself scarce among the foliage.

The flying squirrel was hardly bigger than a chipmunk, but it looked larger in the air with its "wings" unfurled and its bushy tail stretched out. The sight of it exhilarated me. I had often longed to be able to take to the air like that, and I envied the martins in our backyard. They plummeted out of the sky like black darts, pulled out of their dive at the level of the lilac bush, and coasted a lap or two around the yard before coming in neatly to a two-claw landing on the porch of their small house. I watched them with envy and admiration, sadly aware that I shared nothing of their grace. But the flying squirrel was different. Here was a creature with which I had much in common—legs and arms and teeth and hair—whose ability to take flight seemed the result of a fierce desire in it, a longing that had ultimately made it different from other squirrels. It might not yet be able to skim the treetops, but it was clearly making progress in that direction. Perhaps there was hope for me too. I felt heartened.

Some time later I had another adventure in those woods—one that, far from exhilarating me, left me trembling in a cold sweat.

I was alone in the woods on an afternoon late in the summer. I had found a tree with ripe hackberries and, having an endless appetite for anything edible that grew in the woods, I was gorging on them. I jumped up and grasped a big limb, held on and swung myself up onto it. Oblivious to everything but berries, I ate those within reach and looked for more, making my way higher as I ate.

I had been up in the tree for ten minutes when I saw a devil's walkingstick on the limb where I was sitting. I knocked it away with a shiver of disgust. I had learned to live with a lot of ugly bugs, and I could tolerate most of them. But not the devil's walkingstick. It was my bête noire, and the mere sight of one was enough to give me the spasms. They were obscenely unnatural somehow, like toothpicks that had come to life.

After knocking the walkingstick from my limb high in the hackberry tree I felt a touch of the creeping willies. I looked around me with a suspicious eye, and what I saw made my blood run cold. On the limb within arm's reach of me were dozens of walkingsticks. They had blended so well with the twigs that I had not seen them. All at once I saw the awful truth—every branch and twig of the tree was infested with them. There were thousands of them on every side, everywhere I looked. And they *moved*—waving their toothpick legs in a slow, mechanical way that was horrible to see. Every twig was alive!

A cold sweat broke out on my face with a spasm of horror, gooseflesh crawled over my arms and legs and back, and I flung myself out of the tree with a wild abandon, shredding my skin and tearing my clothes on the rough bark, and dislodging a host of walkingsticks on my way to the ground.

When I was out of the tree I flailed at my clothes, my hair, and my back with convulsive panic and got away from there as fast as I could. By the time I got home I had myself under control and was just a little shaky and weak in the knees. As long as I didn't think about it I was all right. But the memory of that shock of awareness that had come in the tree could make me sweat and tremble.

I didn't tell anybody about that moment of horror. In fact, I have never mentioned it to a soul, because there never seemed to be an appropriate time to bring it up. But the main reason I kept silent is that it was too awful for words.

12 DEEP LEAVES

ON OCTOBER MORNINGS the first rays of the sun came through the window and painted the walls with a golden red light that matched the flaming oak logs in the fireplace. From the porch you could see the valley through the purple mist, and the scene was framed by yellow walnut and hickory leaves garnished with frozen dew. The air would be sharp with wood smoke and the smell of breakfast.

Out in the woods along the bluff, possum grapes hung in black clusters, sweetened by frost, and chinkapins on hard-to-find trees drew us to them through waist-deep drifts of leaves. A kind of small tree that grew in the high woods and on the rocky slopes under the bluff—and that oddly enough is a member of the honeysuckle family—bore clusters of blackhaws at the end of every twig. They were hardly as big as raisins and were mostly skin and seeds, which had to be spit out when you ate them. But the middle layer had a dark, sugary taste that I liked. They were no kin to redhaws, despite their name, for redhaws are members of the rose family, and their fruit looks like a miniature apple and tastes a bit like an apple.

The hackberry, unlike those I have mentioned, is a forest-size tree, a member of the elm family that grows to a considerable height. One hackberry tree would have more berries than I could eat in a season. But the most common and plentiful and easily found of all the things to eat in the woods was the persimmon. The soil must have suited them perfectly, for the trees grew everywhere, and persimmon sprouts could take over an abandoned field in a single growing season. Persimmons made a feast for the birds and small game, and sometimes for people too. But as anybody who has ever eaten one knows, they are rich in tannic acid, and only after a frost has turned them to sugar are they fit to eat. But the change that makes them edible also makes them too soft and mushy to store and transport. So as far as I know, persimmons have never been marketed in this country. If you are of an experimental turn, you can fill a ten-gallon crock with ripe persimmons and let them ferment and make persimmon wine. Dad tried it once.

It was too bad that a tree so prolific and well suited to the land as the persimmon had no commercial value. I have learned that the persimmon is the only living relative of the ebony tree, and that the persimmon's black heartwood is used to make golf-club heads. Only the big persimmon trees have such heartwood. The rest of the wood is weak and rots so quickly that it is good for nothing. The large trees with their potentially valuable heartwood were mostly cut down and burned, and thus wasted, as was much of the area's rich timber resources. It was common for barnyard fence posts to be solid walnut, and many great ash and white oak trees were hacked into cross ties that were sold to the railroad for fifty cents apiece.

The black walnut is a tall, handsome tree that can hold its own among oaks and hickories. There were many of them, and they bore tons of walnuts, most of which rotted on the ground. As far as I know, man and squirrels are the only creatures that eat walnuts. Unlike persimmons, which are propagated when their seeds are swallowed and dispersed by animals, walnuts are not meant to be eaten. They are made to lie on the ground, protected by their hulls, saturated in tannic acid. During a winter the hull rots away, while the hard inner shell protects the seed until the growing season. By then it has settled into the ground and the shell has weakened enough for the seed to germinate and take root.

There was a market for black walnuts, and my brother and I were in the walnut business for a while, before we were old enough to know better. There was a catch to it, as there always was when money changed hands: the walnuts had to be hulled before they could be sold. The green hulls are half an inch thick, and nature did not mean for them to be separated from the rest of the walnut. You can cut off the hull with a knife, or you can break it off in chunks with your fingers, but any way you do it, it is slow and tedious work. My brother and I used a walnut huller that Dad made for us. It was like a low wooden stool with an inch-and-a-half hole in the top board. You could put a walnut over the hole and drive it through with a blow of a hammer and strip off most of the hull. But the rest still had to be broken off by hand.

The hulls were saturated with a dark and indelible dye that stained our hands a deep, rich brown. Nothing we could find would take it off. Not kerosene or gasoline. Not even Grandma's lye soap had any effect on it. At school you could tell which boys had been hulling walnuts by looking at their hands. The stain wore off in a week or two, however, and had no ill effects.

The money we got for the sacks of walnuts we hulled couldn't have amounted to more than five cents an hour, and while our time wasn't worth much in any case, my brother and I stopped selling them and hulled only enough for our own use.

Hickory nuts were as plentiful as walnuts and easier to gather. Their outer hulls broke away cleanly, but their inner shell was hard and thick. Both varieties of hickory nut—the ordinary hickory and the scaly-bark hickory—were good to eat, but the latter had bigger nuts and were easier to break open.

Sassafras, like the persimmon, was so common that its sprouts were a nuisance in the field. Its roots and inner bark, cut up and dried, make an aromatic tea that is supposed to be good for you. We kept some dried sassafras in a sack in the kitchen because Grandma was fond of it. There are many things worse to drink than sassafras tea. It is even sold in stores, I believe.

Grandma liked to get things out of the woods, and she knew

everything that was edible. I can see her preparing to lead a blackberry excursion. She always wore a long dress and long stockings, so she needed no extra protection below her waist. But a trip through the blackberry patch called for her sunbonnet—a bonnet like that worn by the faceless figure on a box of Old Dutch cleanser, the kind of bonnet with starched flat sidepieces like blinders and a ruffled hood in front. Next she would pull a pair of long cotton stockings over her arms, after having cut holes in them for her fingers, and thus armored against the elements she would take pail in hand and, seeing that we boys were equipped with pails, sally forth toward the blackberries. The best patch was a quarter of a mile from our house, at the head of a ravine at the edge of the woods. Here grew a mass of thorny blackberry vines impenetrable to everything but rabbits and Grandma.

Grandma's precautions had been taken to protect her from the sun, the briars, and chiggers. My brother and I scorned such measures as unmanly and paid the price of ignorance. Sun and briars were nothing to us, but we were always having to learn anew about chiggers. Perhaps because they were too small to see, we would forget about the misery they could cause, and while they were apt to be lurking anywhere in the grass or bushes, they were certain to be in the blackberry patch. You could count on it.

Some of the things we ate in the woods I have never seen elsewhere and don't even know a standard name for. What we called "ground apricots" were nothing like apricots. They were walnut-size globes that grew on vines on the ground. When they were ripe they were light brown and wrinkled. Inside the papery shell were dozens of seeds coated with a sweet-tasting pulp that had a unique aroma. And our "ground cherries" were a small, berry-like fruit that grew inside a delicate little paper lantern on a low shrub.

Poke plants grew everywhere, in and out of the woods. Their

early shoots look a bit like asparagus spears and have served as table food—either as a salad or boiled like spinach—in some parts of the South for generations. Grandma claimed to like poke and tried to promote it, but while Mother and Dad would go along with her, my brother and I never pretended to find it edible. I always thought it was a shame that we were urged to eat poke greens, which look and taste like boiled weeds, but were unable to eat the berries from the same plant. Poke berries grow in tempting clusters of red-purple hue at the top of the mature plant. They look delicious, but their taste is not good—except to birds perhaps.

The most delicious of all these wild products was the mushroom, or morels, as they are more properly called. Of these there were three kinds—red, brown, and white—which all tasted alike. They could be found only in early spring, in the brief spell when the sun is warm before the leaves come out. The sunlight coming full through the still bare limbs of the trees would bring the morels out of the rotten wood around the base of stumps or fallen logs, where their spores had lodged. They were scarce, however. Dad found a few of them every spring, but though I spent hours in the woods searching for them I never found more than one or two. Most are no bigger than a saltshaker, but the red ones could be much bigger. Mrs. Troutman, who lived in the woods on the north end of the mountain and came to help Mother on washdays, once brought us a red mushroom as big as a pineapple, which she had found on her way to our house. Mother sliced it and fried it with batter for our dinner at noon, and there was enough for all of us.

Dad grew sweet potatoes for our home use. One Saturday every fall was spent getting them in. First we pulled away the vines that covered the ground in the sweet potato patch, then Dad hitched both his horses to the turning plow and went down the rows plowing as deep as he could. The plow turned up a heavy ribbon of earth that broke as it fell over. The ground had to be just right, neither too wet nor too dry, to dig sweet potatoes. While he was plowing, my brother and I would walk down to the mailbox for our mail. There was seldom much mail, but there was always a copy of our newspaper, *The Muskogee Phoenix,* to which Dad subscribed.

The Meadows house, down by the mailbox, usually showed some sign of life, but it would be silent and empty on a Saturday, everybody gone to town. We would retrace our steps back up the mountain road with the newspaper, through the woods where the silence was broken only by the caw of crows or the raucous jays. By the time we got back Dad would be through plowing and ready to get the sweet potatoes out. It was a dirty job but a rewarding one. We went down the furrows on our knees, pulled out the sweet potatoes, and threw them into buckets. Some would be laid bare completely, and some would be partly uncovered. Others would be cut in two by the plow and showed bright gold spots in the dirt. We could finish the job by noon, having dug up maybe four or five bushels.

Next Dad would hitch the team of horses to the wagon, and we would bring the sweet potatoes into the barn and carry the baskets up to the house and leave them in the yard. By now we would be hungry, and on days when the women were gone Dad would fix us something. He wasn't much of a cook, however, and with him in charge the noon meal was apt to be something like cold ham and biscuits.

We spent the afternoon washing the sweet potatoes, which always came out of the ground with dirt clinging to them. We did this in the yard near the house, where we had access to washtubs and water from the house tank. We filled three tubs with water and put the sweet potatoes through them in a regular sequence— one to wash off the chunks of dirt, the next to rub them clean, and the third to rinse them off. When they were clean we spread them on the grass to dry in the sun while we cleaned out the tubs.

By the middle of the afternoon the morning breeze had died away, and the sunlight was a clear golden tint on the leaves of the maple trees. Far off in the woods crows kept up an endless conference about matters I never understood.

All the things we found to eat in the woods had grown there for centuries. And centuries ago, for thousands of years, people had come there in the fall, because that was a time of plenty. They came in small bands—of fifteen to thirty, perhaps—to camp near the springs in the woods below the bluff. Sometimes they stayed through the winter, and in the spring, when the flood season was over, they returned to the more populous river valleys with as many deerskin as they could carry. They did not live there in summer because they could never see the sun.

For those ancient people the season of falling leaves held terrors of its own, terrors we do not understand because we can never experience them. But in their time the great climax forest of deciduous trees was unbroken, and when the multitudes of oaks and hickories and maples and ash were stripped to bare branches, their leaves lay on the ground in incalculable masses. The wind swept them out of the high woods in great clouds, mingling yellow and red and brown, and heaped them in drifts fifty feet deep in the lee of the bluffs. Autumn winds raised leaf storms that buried trails and marks and filled the stream beds from bank to bank.

For the small fur-bearing animals it was a time of peril and affliction. The shy bluff dwellers had to burrow half a day to find water. The noise of the leaves in the windy forest was a constant hissing and scraping and rustling that could grow to a roaring tumult. It drowned any sound of an approaching predator.

Fire from lightning could spread at the speed of the wind and bring panic and catastrophe. A spirit of terror reigned in the woods in the season of deep leaves, affecting every animal. Even the panther, who had least to fear, would return to his cave after a night in the gusty woods to find its entrance buried under a flood of oak and hickory leaves. He prowled restlessly and slept badly until the spell was broken at last by a cold misty rain or a storm of sleet as winter approached.

For us, all that was left of the ancient season of fear and madness was a full moon of Halloween and a kind of wild lonesomeness in the fall of the year. I was never lonesome on dark, dreary days in winter, or in the long, hot, silent summer afternoons when the grasshoppers filled the air with their alien stitch. But on those bright October days when the air was cool and crystal clear and the sunlight flamed in the maple leaves, I sometimes felt that we were trapped in a spell and cut off from the world forever. If Mother and Grandma were gone for the day it seemed doubly lonesome, because my brother and Dad were affected too, and even when we were working together we didn't talk much. It takes at least four people to keep the deepest kind of lonesomeness away.

By supper time the sweet potatoes would be clean and dry and ready to put away. Most of them we stored in the cellar, but some went up in the attic under the eaves. Now Grandma and Mother would be home, busy in the kitchen, and we finished our chores with the feeling of having done a good day's work.

The evenings were long and quiet. Sometimes we listened to a radio program on our battery-powered radio. But often we would just sit, talking sometimes, while each of us did whatever he felt like doing. We seldom had visitors in the evening and hardly ever went anywhere.

One autumn night along toward bedtime, we were all in the

front room of our house on Coon Mountain—Grandma at work on one of her embroidery-picture projects, Dad and my brother reading, Mother doing something with needle and thread, and me busy with one of the model airplanes that were the ruination of a once-decent card table—when something happened that made us all stop what we were doing and hold our breath.

The cause was something too incredible to be frightening, at first. Like the first tremor of an earthquake—the sound of footsteps overhead. We had not been talking, so nobody had to say *shh!* or *listen!* The sound was unmistakable. I looked at Dad and saw him lift his eyes from his paper and take his pipe from his mouth. He looked at Mother. I looked at Grandma. She looked at Dad. Everybody's eyes went from one to another, confirming what we had heard and silently asking for some explanation. Nobody spoke.

The sound that froze us in our places had been an unmistakable *thump!*, followed a few seconds later by another *thump!*, and even while we exchanged glances there was another *thump*. The sounds proceeded regularly in one direction and seemed to come from a spot in the ceiling directly above Dad's chair. The steps were moving along the length of the house, from east to west, in the attic: *thump . . . thump . . . thump . . .* at intervals of several seconds.

My heart began to beat rapidly. I didn't sense any danger in the sounds. What frightened me was the realization that none of the grown-ups knew what was making them. Grandma was the first to speak. Her voice conveyed amazement and a trace of fear. Mother seemed frightened. Dad shook his head and listened. I could sense his astonishment and wonder as he looked up at the ceiling. The *thump*s had passed over his head and were moving along toward the attic stairs.

Dad got up quietly and left the room. We heard his steps on the stairs to the attic. Soon he came back and motioned to us all to move over to the north side of the room. Not knowing why, we did as he wanted, then we heard him go back upstairs again. There was the sudden *bang!* of a rifle shot, and we heard Dad exclaim, "Damn!" Then there was a brief silence, and we could tell that the thumping had stopped.

Dad put away the rifle and flashlight that he had been using and came back to the front room. The thumps we had heard, he explained to us, were made by something we could never have guessed or foreseen. A big rat had got into the house and, finding the sweet potatoes stored upstairs, had decided to take one home with it. The sweet potato was bigger than the rat, but the rat had managed to pull it up over the floor joists, back under the eaves where there was no flooring. Every eighteen inches, as the rat pulled the sweet potato over a joist, it fell onto the sheetrock of the ceiling with a thump.

Dad had managed to get a shot at the rat with his .22 rifle, shooting between the joists while he stood on the stairs. But the flashlight had alarmed the rodent and he got away scot-free and unscathed, leaving the sweet potato laying there between the joists.

13 WILD HONEY

ON MISTY FALL DAYS my thoughts go back to the mountain, and I can smell the blue smoke from a fire of oak chips and hear the slow, soft drops of foggy dew that collect on the tree limbs and fall on the dead leaves.

On a day like this Dad and his friend Henry, who lived a mile away on the north end of the mountain, went to get the honey from a bee tree they had found in the woods below the spring. They built a fire at the base of the hollow tree and smothered the flames with bark and chips of green wood to smoke out the bees. Then they took turns with a heavy, double-bitted axe chopping at the tree, a tough old red oak two or three feet thick. It was hard work, and they were sweating at it for quite a while. The sound of axe blows echoed flatly from the bluff and died in the wet woods.

We three boys—my brother and I and Henry's son, Floyd— lurked in the underbrush, excited and fidgety, dodging the bees and the big oak chips that whirred out wildly at every blow of the axe. The men had ordered us to stay back—far back out of range. But the thought of getting honey out of an oak tree was too appealing. Nothing could have kept us away. We wrestled and scrambled on the brushy hillside, always edging closer to the bee tree, and tried to watch the men's progress without calling attention to ourselves.

Dad kept an eye on us, and when the tree swayed and gave a loud creak, he waved us back. The big red oak went down with a majestic crash, taking a mass of grapevine and saplings with it into ruin. The bees had already abandoned it.

The tree lay sprawled down the hillside, but we couldn't get at the honey until Dad had chopped a hole in the hollow trunk. Then we clambered over its still-leafy branches, crowded up close, and looked in, where we could see big strips of honeycomb stuck to the inner wall of the trunk, all the little hexagonal cells neatly sealed with wax to hold the honey. It looked like we had struck gold. There must have been enough honey in the tree to fill a washtub.

Dad reached in, carefully detached a long slab of honeycomb, and lifted it out. He broke it apart and handed each of us a piece. We sank our teeth into the dripping, waxy chunks as the honey ran down our chins and up our arms under our sleeves. We tasted the thick sweetness of it and chewed the wax.

The honey tasted different, we could tell at once. Then we began to realize that it wasn't just different, it was *very* different, different in the wrong way. It was *awfully* different! I spat out the mass of beeswax and kept spitting in my efforts to get the lingering taste of it off my tongue. The other boys and the men were spitting in every direction, and for a minute nobody said anything. Then Dad wiped his mouth with the back of his hand and said, "Dogfennel!"

Dogfennel is a modest weed with little yellow flowers that all animals, including boys, soon learned to avoid. It is not a poisonous weed, but its taste is vile and bitter. The worst of its bitterness is that it lingers on your tongue and fills your mouth with its awful flavor for hours, even days. One small petal of dogfennel flower on your tongue will leave its memory for life. Sometimes a careless cow would munch a sprig of dogfennel, and that little mistake would spoil her milk.

The bees had the last laugh. They would be able to salvage most of their hoard, which was no good to us. We left it in the tree and plodded home through the dripping October woods with our empty buckets and the vile taste of dogfennel between our teeth. Dad grumbled about the bees and couldn't understand what they had thought they were doing. Most bees leave dogfennel alone. These were wild bees, however, and had taken whatever they found. A trashy class of bees! And lazy, too. There was plenty of clover not half a mile away, if they had taken the trouble to look for it.

We never had to go without honey, however, that year or any other. Dad kept three or four hives of bees on a stand under the big walnut tree between the house and the barn. His bees were always busy, of course. They worked seven days a week, and they knew better than to try slipping any dogfennel over on us. They were a bit of an affliction to us boys; we all had to get stung a few times before we could learn how far to go with them. But we didn't resent them as we resented the wasps, because we knew that when the summer was over Dad would make them pay for their arrogance and hostile moves.

Robbing the bees was a yearly event in which we had no part except as interested bystanders. Dad's preparations were elaborate and conveyed the impression that this was not just another chore but a campaign. He prepared for it by firing up his smoker—a storebought device like a coffee can with a small bellows on one side. He put burning rags into the can and closed the lid, and by squeezing the handle on the bellows forced air into the bottom and a thick stream of smoke out of the funnel-like spout on the lid. For his own protection he tied the cuffs of his pants over his shoe tops with binder twine to keep bees from crawling up his legs, and he spread a piece of mosquito net over his hat and tucked it into his collar all around before buttoning his shirt. The last step was to draw on his gloves and get somebody to button his shirt cuffs over them.

Thus prepared, and as bee-proof as he could make himself, he took the smoker in one hand and a clean dishpan in the other and set out to do a job on the bees. The rest of us kept our distance, Mother and Grandma talking in subdued voices as they tried to keep an eye on me and my brother and worry about Dad in among the bees. He always got stung a few times. Sometimes the smoke would be so thick we couldn't see what he was doing, then we would catch sight of him flailing his long butcher knife and stamping his feet, or fogging away at the bees and muttering and cussing to himself.

Half an hour later he would emerge from the battle smoke, in a mood that varied by the number of times he had got stung, with his dishpan full of golden honeycomb oozing honey made from clover blossoms and peach nectar and other delicious things. I am no gourmet, but the honey sold in stores has no appeal to me unless it bears the bodies of a few bees who gave their lives to defend it.

The bees always survived Dad's raids, and eventually they multiplied until there were too many bees for our hives. Then they would split up and half would take off with a new queen to find another home. If we were lucky enough to spot the new swarm while it was assembling, we could get them into a new hive and add to our stands. But this was a tricky maneuver and we never knew how it would turn out.

One fine spring day Mother, who had been hanging out clothes in the backyard, came hurrying into the house in a flutter, saying the bees were swarming. Grandma heard this and took charge at once. She sent my brother racing off to the field for Dad while she directed my mother and me in a holding operation to keep the bees from getting away to the woods. She thrust dishpans and heavy spoons into our hands and, equipping herself the same way, hustled us out into the yard, where the bees were swarming in a fuzzy cloud about ten feet above the ground. They made a high, sustained droning as they drifted slowly toward the woods.

Grandma banged on her dishpan with her ladle and yelled at us to do the same. "They won't sting you while they're a-swarming!" she declared, and stood boldly under the cloud of bees, making a loud racket.

I had to do as Grandma ordered, even if my heart wasn't in it. I had recently advanced to that brilliant stage of childhood that comes when we realize that older people don't know everything. But I still knew enough to keep my mouth shut and follow orders, and I stood out in the yard feeling like a fool and banging on my dishpan while Mother and Grandma did the same. Mother trusted Grandma's knowledge in such matters because Grandma had lived through the Reconstruction in western Arkansas and knew a thing or two about surviving. I, of course, had doubts about the present applicability of such ancient lore.

The three of us kept banging away on the pans, and at first the bees seemed oblivious to the uproar. Then they rose higher and drifted around the end of the house, where they paused to regroup under the gable. We followed, staying as close to the bees as we could, and soon the cloud of bees came down to a few feet above our heads and hovered uncertainly as it moved toward an old apple tree on the terrace behind our house. The cloudy, droning mass of bees enveloped one of the apple tree's stout branches and appeared to be condensing around it. Then we could see the limb blacken and swell as the bees came to rest on it and on each other. The swelling cluster grew quickly, and by the time Dad and my brother arrived the bees were all in a solid clump on the apple tree like a big black hornet's nest made of the living bodies of thousands of bees.

Grandma made us keep up the clanging with our pans while Dad brought some sawhorses and boards and quickly set up a low scaffold under the limb where the bees clung. He brought a spare box hive and placed it on the scaffold. Then he hit the limb of the apple tree with a fence post hard enough to jar the bees loose. The whole swarming mass fell onto the box hive in a lump that melted away into its innumerable bee components. It was an odd sight.

At this, Grandma stopped her banging and lowered her ladle and pan, like a conductor lowering his baton at the end of a performance. The bees checked out the box and found it acceptable, and a few days later Dad moved them back to the beehive stands under the walnut tree.

Grandma was pleased, and while she was the most modest and unassuming of ladies, it was clear she felt much of the credit belonged to her. Nobody would have dreamed of challenging her methods—not after such a clear demonstration of their effectiveness.

I kept my mouth shut, of course, but it was hard for me to believe that banging on dishpans could have any effect on bees except to make them want to flee the place. I know that there is a scientific explanation for what happened. But at the time I knew even less about science than I knew about bees, and the most likely explanation I could see was that God had intervened on Grandma's behalf. I knew no more about God than I knew about bees or science, but I had at least heard of Him and knew that He worked in mysterious ways. It stood to reason that He would be on Grandma's side, because she was very devout and was always reading the Bible.

Grandma liked the Bible and *Gone with the Wind,* but she thought most printed matter was a lot of foolishness. In this her judgment was sound enough, on the whole, but if she had perused my fifth-grade reader it would have given her something to think about. In it was an interesting article about China, along with a picture of some Chinese peasants standing out in a field beating on what looked like dishpans with sticks and staring up at the sky. The caption explained that here was a fine example of ignorant superstition at work—the peasants were beating on the pans in order to drive away a great dragon that was eating up the sun.

By the grace of God we had no neighbors to see us out in the yard beating on pans and staring up at the sky. I would have been terribly embarrassed if we had been living in town. But to tell the truth I enjoyed the event, because for 364 days out of the year we had to act as if we were in full view of the public.

14 TRAP LINES

OUR HOUSE on Coon Mountain is still occupied, and though I have seen it many times I have not been inside it for forty-five years. If it has the original windows, I could find a small hole in a window frame in the front room. It was drilled in the winter of 1933, so my brother and I could trap snowbirds.

We trapped them in the traditional way, scattering crumbs on the snow and propping a cardboard box over the crumbs on a stick with a string tied to it. The string led through the hole in the window to the living room, where we could watch the trap without freezing our noses. When the snowbirds came hopping along, pecking at the crumbs, one always hopped heedlessly under the box. A quick tug dislodged the prop, and the snowbird was our prisoner, a victim of his own hunger.

There was not much we could do with a snowbird, after we caught it. They were too small to eat and, being more or less harmless, were reluctantly set free. But it was fun to trap them on a cold, snowy day when there was nothing else to do.

We never stayed home from school because of cold weather, although a few times we walked more than a snowy mile only to find that school had been called off. So we would trudge home and take our time about it. Instead of following the road all the way, we would go up through the woods, following the branch to our spring. It was interesting to see the stream frozen in its tracks, with little petrified waterfalls and thick white whorls of ice in its pools, and the hear the water gurgling down below, still flowing. At the pond behind our barn, we would test the ice and find that it bore our weight easily. We arrived at home with red noses, numb of foot and watery-eyed from the cold, our mittens sodden with snow crust.

When we were warm and dry again, we would play in the old barn, in the hay. We made cave houses of bales, heaping loose hay over them, and lurked in them in the dark, eating apples and being secret. The caverns of hay were cold, but they had a dark, wintry mustiness about them that gave them a mysterious appeal.

There was little to lure us into the woods in winter. Dad hunted squirrels and quail, but we were too young for that. Still at the inconsequential stage of childhood, much of what we did now seems pointless. We would spend half a day with Robert Meadows and Floyd, hunting rabbits in the valley. At least we called it hunting, although chasing is a more accurate word for what we did. We had air rifles, but we did little damage with them.

The hunting, such as it was, was done by the dogs. The rabbits lived in the brush piles, which were numerous and everywhere to be found—heaps of sprouts and tree branches, either hewn for firewood or cut down in clearing a field or cleaning out a fence-row. The rabbits ensconced at the heart of a big brush pile were as safe as they could long to be. But if one of them got nervous and tried to get out of the territory, he was in trouble. Pursued by dogs, a rabbit might make the mistake of taking cover in a small brush pile, where he could be seen. We would poke at him mercilessly with sticks until he made another mad scamper for safety, fleeing over the snow with boys and dogs in full cry on his heels.

We caught few rabbits. Very few. Which was just as well, for almost nobody would eat them for fear of getting one that was diseased. The fear was probably groundless, but the unspoken rule against eating rabbits was seldom broken. Nevertheless, we chased them from here to there across Horn Valley, and a cold sport it was, as I recall it. I have never much liked cold-weather sports. I got my fill of skiing before I was eight, which has saved me having to learn at great expense in middle age that I do not like it very much.

An even colder and less noisy sport was trapping. And now that I think about it I don't suppose it was a sport at all. Dad set a few steel traps around the bluff for skunks and possums, which he took for the skins. He was careful to check them often, and sometimes I would offer to do this for him. I would have to go out early in the morning, when the woods and bluffs seemed far away in another world. It was a cold and lonely chore in the gray woods, and the few skins we got were not worth the trouble. But it was something to do.

The only furs worth more than a dollar or two were fox pelts. Foxes are hard to trap, but one winter Dad was bound and determined to trap a fox, and he succeeded. He found a lot of fox tracks in a patch of sandy ground near our orchard, at the head of a ravine, so he set his traps there. But first he hung the traps in a smoky fire, along with a pair of leather gloves that he used while handling the traps. He buried the traps in the sand, just below the surface, with a wad of smoked cotton under the trigger pans. He buried the stakes and chains too, and wearing the leather gloves he brushed away every sign of his presence. He may have sprinkled some kind of lure on the ground, but I don't remember that. Altogether it was a tedious business, but it led to the capture and death of a big red fox.

Dad was satisfied; having proved to himself that he was able to outsmart a fox, he didn't bother them any more. He sent the fox skin off somewhere and had it made into a neckpiece for Mother. It came back all neatly lined with silk and with yellow glass fox eyes that looked real. Whoever made it sewed a snap under its nose that fastened to another snap on its hind foot. Mother was proud of it and looked quite striking with it around her neck.

One year I ran a trap line of my own—a trap line for mice.

There were mice all over the place—in the house and cellar, and in the barn and smokehouse and chickenhouse. We had no cats at the time. The cats we had had on the place never got on well with the dogs, and they tended to kill young chicks and Mother's pet songbirds. Eventually they had drifted off into the woods and a more independent way of life.

My idea was to trap mice systematically, rather than in the off-and-on, here-and-there way they had been trapped before. I got Dad to stake me to a dozen ordinary mousetraps, baited them with bacon scraps, and set them out. I put two in the cellar, two in the attic, two in the kitchen, two on the back porch, and two around the woodpile in the backyard. I caught ten mice on the first night, and when the number fell off I went on to trap the mice in the toolshed and smokehouse. In a couple of weeks the mice population was down to a reasonable level. It would have been impossible to rid the place of them permanently. They kept moving in out of the woods and fields in winter.

I skinned a few of the mice, but I soon stopped because I couldn't find anything to do with their skins. I felt that was a shame, because mouse fur is beautifully soft and silky.

The last animal I trapped was a groundhog. I did not trap it out of wanton idleness but for a purpose, as I will explain.

I was always trying to make things. More often than not my ideas turned out to be impractical, but I kept trying, and I always had my eye out for something I could make use of. One summer Dad reshingled our house, and when he had used up a keg of shingle nails I asked him to give me the empty keg. When he asked me what I wanted it for I told him I wanted it to put things in. That was not true, however. I kept my real reason from Dad because I could tolerate suspicion easier than I could accept the scornful skepticism my ideas usually evoked.

I wanted the nail keg to make a drum. I had hankered for a drum for a long time but had never found anything to make one out of. The nail keg looked right. It was made of good strong hickory staves banded with steel hoops, with an iron rim around the top. It was about eighteen inches high.

Now I needed something for a drumhead. I tried everything I could lay my hands on—canvas, leather, rubber from an old inner tube. No matter how tight I stretched it, the most I could get was a hopeless thump that couldn't be heard any distance at all.

I was twelve at the time and not easily discouraged. I kept my eyes open and eventually got exactly what I needed. Over in the alfalfa field near the bluff, a big groundhog had grown lazy and careless and moved out of the woods, digging his burrow in the field where we could hardly miss it. So I trapped him and skinned him and made a drumhead out of his hide.

That sounds easy, if you say it fast. And in truth the first step is pretty routine for a boy of twelve. The other two steps are not.

What I mean is this. You can trap an animal and shoot it without getting involved with it directly, but skinning it is a direct, hands-on experience. There is no other way. Skinning it is a matter of flesh and blood and guts, and the smell of those things, along with the sight and smell of half-digested alfalfa in its stomach and digestive tract—all of which make the animal very real to you. It is good training for anyone suffering from an overly sensitive concern for the rights and feelings of others, because if you are going to finish the job you have to set aside your squeamishness and get on with it.

I cut open the groundhog's skin lengthwise along the middle of its belly, and not having any skill at this I made the cut too deep. There was not much between the groundhog's skin and its stomach, so the contents of its stomach were soon in my way. I had to take a firm grip on myself and get on with what I was doing, slitting the skin down the inner sides of its legs and peeling the skin back around its ribs and up over its head. There was no way to do that neatly. It was not pretty, but I had to be satisfied with the bloody mass of hair and hide I finally came away with.

That was the messiest part of the job, but not the nastiest. After getting rid of the corpse, I buried the fresh hide in a hole beside the ash pile near the house. I put a bucketful of ashes into the hole on top of the hide and poured in a bucketful of water before I filled the hole back up with dirt.

Three days later when I took the hide out of the hole, it was ready to be scraped. It was more than ready. I'm sure you would not have liked the looks of it any more than the smell. (Mother and Grandma did not wait for me to ask their opinion of it.) After the skinning ordeal, I could endure the smell of the hide easily enough and soon got used to it, but out of respect for others' feelings I took it out to the woods to work on. I easily scraped off the hair, and when I had washed off the dirt and ashes I had a good thick piece of rawhide. I scraped it some more with a knife, to take off the bits of flesh and fat that had come off with the skin, and kept at it until the piece was clean, by my standards.

I laid the still wet and stretchable groundhog hide over the open end of the nail keg and cut around the side, leaving two or three inches hanging over, and cut holes all around the edge of the piece. Most drums have two heads, but since I had only one groundhog I had to make it do. I cut the scraps of rawhide into narrow strips and was ready to lace on the drumhead. I drove shingle nails into the wooden bottom, hooked the lacing over the nail heads, and drew it tight.

It was not a drum that would have won any prizes. I cherish the memory of it because it was the first thing I ever made that turned out to be more or less what I wanted. At least the reality of it bore some resemblance to what I'd had in mind as I worked.

The rawhide of the laces and drumhead shrank as it dried, over the period of two or three days. The thick, smelly groundhog skin was stretched so taut that it became as thin and hard as parchment. When I tapped it with a padded stick it gave off a reverberating medium-deep drumlike tone. It never completely lost its original smell, and its tone was perhaps not as deep and reverberating as I might have wished, but it had that true, drumlike quality of sound, and that was the main thing. It might not have stirred a red man's soul, but if beaten long enough it could get on the nerves of white men and women a hundred yards away.

15 CORN PLANTER

DAD'S COLLECTION of antique farm machinery included a device that looked like a plow with an iron canister mounted above the plowshares and supported on two wheels at the sides. The canister was fitted on the inside with a perforated iron disk at the bottom, which turned slowly on a gear connected to the axle of the wheels. The canister held about half a bushel of seed corn, which dropped through the holes in the disk into an iron tube and fell to the ground in a furrow, to be covered up by another small plowshare mounted behind. It was a primitive machine, but it worked well enough. With it, one man and a horse could plant as much corn in a day as four men could working by hand.

It was a good thing that the planter saved labor, because everything else about the crop was hard work. That is to say, it used to be so when it was raised in our part of the country.

The Cherokees knew little about the business of farming. They and the southern whites who intermarried and came west with them knew how to grow cotton and corn and a few vegetables. But they were subsistence farmers, and such matters as market price and soil suitability were remote from their ken. The Indian Territory land was poor crop land, for the most part. A year or two of cotton or corn was all it was worth. They eventually stopped trying to grow cotton, since it wasn't good for anything except money, and if you couldn't make money from it there was no point in growing it. Corn, however, they wouldn't give up. They would plant a patch of corn here one year, and there the next, a few acres at least. Because corn is the staff of life. If you can grow corn, you will stay alive, no matter how much money you don't have. There are so many things you can do with corn.

Dad liked to plant corn on his birthday, the twenty-fifth of March. That is early in the year, but the corn doesn't mind the cold weather if you don't. It is perfectly content to lie there in the ground until it is time for it to come up. After planting the corn, Dad could forget about it for a while. By the end of April the little green tubelike corn plants would be four inches high. Before long the weeds and grass would start to creep in among them. Corn needs all the nourishment it can get from the ground, so the grass and weeds had to be kept out of the corn by hoeing.

In our part of the country hoeing corn was the birthright—or the curse of Adam, depending on how you look at it—of every boy. Girls were exempt usually, and a girl who had to hoe corn was felt to be much imposed upon. But all boys were considered eligible after the age of eight.

While it is true that a nine-year-old boy is quite capable of hoeing corn, he is not fully capable of understanding the necessity of it and the value of it, and so is not able to get much satisfaction out of it or take much joy in it. Such a boy is apt to regard a cornfield the way a convict regards the road he labors to build.

Everybody raised some corn, but nobody raised a lot. Some hoed their corn twice, some hoed it but once. Whether they hoed it once or twice depended on the size of their family and the weather, especially the timing of the rain, which often favored the weeds and Johnsongrass more than the corn. In the middle of the summer they plowed between the rows with a cultivator plow to throw dirt up over the exposed roots and cover any newly sprouted weeds. This was called laying a crop by. When the corn was laid by you didn't have to work it any more until it was time to pick it in the fall.

That didn't mean you didn't have to worry about it. Any number of things could happen to it—although there was nothing you could do about them but fret. For one thing, it might not rain after the Fourth of July, in which case the crop would just dry up and dwindle away. But you might get fifteen inches of rain in August. You might go out to the field one day and find every tall cornstalk lying green and flat on the ground with its shallow roots naked in the air. There was always the chance of hail stripping the stalks bare. And too much rain in the fall could turn the hard, golden ears of corn to a smutty black mess. All in all, corn was a fussy crop.

The job of picking corn went best with four workers—one to drive the team hitched to the wagon, and three to pull the ears and throw them into the wagon. Since the rows were only three feet apart, the wagon had to drive over a row as it went along, leaving the cornstalks crushed down. The man who had to pick in the "down row" had to stoop to his work constantly, so the workers took turns at it.

Corn was picked late in the fall, after all the other crops had been got out of the way. By then the plants were all dry and their hard, bladelike leaves were sharp. You could try picking corn without gloves, but by the end of the day your hands would be lacerated and too sore to do anything the next day. It was best to wear gloves, even if your hands were callused and tough to start with. There was also dust and pollen in the cornfield that rubbed into your skin and made some people's eyelids swell painfully.

The job went best with four men, as I have said, but we never had that many. We never grew more than four or five acres of corn, and Dad used to pick the crop himself sometimes. He would tie the horse's reins to the brake pole of the wagon and start and stop the team by command. That takes a lot of conviction and a voice with authority in it. After my brother and I were old enough to help him, one of us would drive the wagon while the other pulled corn. Dad would pull two rows to our one. One year the weather turned cold before we had the corn picked, and Dad built a fire at the edge of the field so we could warm our hands and feet after every round.

Six months passed between the planting and the picking. But in spite of all the work it involved we liked to grow corn. The work in the field was only one side of the matter, however. There were two other sides—preparing it and eating it.

I have always liked any food made with corn—everything from tortillas to corn dogs. It has been so with me from my childhood. In summer we ate boiled corn on the cob every day. Those roasting ears, as we called them, came from the garden rather than the field. They have always been my favorite food. As soon as I had my first set of teeth, I learned the price of gluttony by eating, I am told, eight ears of corn on the cob with butter and salt. My stomach rose in rebellion then, but the experience only brought my fondness down to a more reasonable level.

Corn bread too was a part of our daily fare, winter and summer. Everybody ate corn bread. There were as many varieties of it as there were of people who prepared it, but there were two basic kinds and people liked one or the other, but not both. The first kind was baked on a kind of sheet and came out of the oven flat and hard and a light tan color tending to whitish. It had a bitter taste to it that I did not like, which probably came from mixing soda or baking powder with the cornmeal. This was the kind of corn bread Mother's family ate, and it was the only kind her father liked. Dad's family liked the other kind, however, and in this regard Mother had changed her tastes and cooking habits to please him.

The second kind of corn bread, the kind we ate, was baked in a black iron skillet. The batter included milk and eggs and a bit of sugar to take off the bitterness of the baking powder. It came out of the oven with a rich, deep brown crust and was served in thick wedges like pieces of pie that could be cut open and buttered and eaten with almost anything.

A meal might include roasting ears, corn bread, and perch rolled in cornmeal and fried. Between the field and the table, however, was another sequence of laborious tasks. When an ear of corn is gathered it still has the shuck on it. It is usually dry, but even the driest corn has some moisture in it and must be stored so the air can circulate through it, in a crib of some kind without solid walls.

Some of the corn went to the chickens, but before even the chickens could eat it there was work to be done—boy's work, at this stage, which my brother and I did every day. We would get a bushel of dried ears from the crib and, after tearing off the shucks, we'd throw the yellow ears into a tub. Next we hauled out the corn sheller. This was a cast-iron tool that clamped onto the side of the tub. It looked a bit like a sausage grinder, with a crank handle and an opening on top where the corn was put in. The handle was bolted onto an iron disk a foot in diameter studded with dozens of iron teeth, which grated against the ear of corn and tore off the hard yellow kernels when the handle was cranked. It was hard work, but the grains of corn rattled into the tub with a cheerful, productive sound. They looked like nuggets of gold and were dry and hard and cool to the touch. The shelled corn had all the smells in it—the smell of fields and shucks and cobs and stalks condensed and mingled. A bushel of ears came to only a gallon of shelled corn. But all the work to this point— planting and hoeing and plowing and picking and shucking and shelling—had been aimed at this.

The animals got a share, but some of the best shelled corn went into making hominy. This was Grandma's special field. Mother could do it, and she helped Grandma, but she didn't really enjoy making hominy as much as Grandma did. Since the boys' part was done when the corn was shelled, all I know about making hominy is from watching Grandma at work.

Hominy making is by no means a lost art, and there are plenty of authorities on the subject. My impression is that it was an outdoor task that took the better part of a week. Still, I always regarded Grandma's hominy making as time well spent.

She would put a couple of gallons of shelled corn into a big black iron pot in the backyard and leave it to soak in lye water. Some people bought lye in cans, but Grandma knew how to make lye water of wood ashes—a messy process indeed. After it had soaked two or three days, the grains of corn would have swelled to two or three times their size and split open their thin transparent husks.

When it had soaked long enough, she drained the lye water and washed the corn two or three times, rubbing the grains between her palms to take off the split husks—another tedious and time-consuming chore, but one the hominy maker was judged by. A husk that remained, or even a piece of one, would eventually get into somebody's mouth and lodge between his teeth and be just cause for complaint.

When the grains were all clean and free of husks, Grandma was ready to make hominy. She filled the kettle again with fresh water and built a fire under it. The hot water drew out whatever lye remained in the grains. When the kettle was drained once more the hominy was ready to pack into jars and dip in boiling water before being sealed. Canned this way it would keep indefinitely.

I have described what I remember of hominy making only to give an idea of the amount of time-consuming work that was connected to every step of the corn business as I knew it. All the labor has been taken out of corn today, of course.

The only corn food we didn't eat was hominy grits, which are made of cracked corn rather than whole grains. Grandma looked on grits as low-class, because if you made grits you didn't have all the work of slipping the husks by hand.

Along with the garden corn and field corn Dad planted a few rows of popcorn every year. It had to be shelled by hand because the ears were too small for the cornsheller. We shelled it by rubbing one ear against another. There were few things better than popcorn with fresh butter and salt.

The only dish made of corn which I have never been much excited about is mush. This is nothing more then cornmeal boiled with a little salt. Grandma's generation seemed to like it, and we had it occasionally on our table. But it was too bland for me. If more mush was cooked than was eaten, you could look forward to having fried mush the next day—cold mush formed into little patties and fried in a skillet. If it has a crust you can crunch your teeth into, with butter and salt it is not bad.

Nobody has ever found much commercial use for corn shucks and corncobs. After all, there is a demand for only so many hot tamales and corncob pipes. Corncobs littered every barnyard until they decayed. If dry they would burn, but not well. The same is true of the cornstalks, which were left in the fields, where they rattled on windy nights with a ghostly sound, and after a winter snow they seemed to stand shivering in the cold fields, tattered and forlorn.

16 NIGHT HUNTERS

A COLD, STILL EVENING in winter, when darkness falls before the chores are done and we eat our supper by yellow lamplight. Dad has been working around the place all day, and now he rests and smokes his pipe by the fire. Out in the kitchen Mother and Grandma are still washing the supper dishes. The quietness is broken by our dogs barking in the front yard. They bark noisily but in a polite kind of way, announcing a friendly visitor. Soon we hear heavy footsteps on the front porch and a man's voice calling out, "Hello!" Then the front door opens and in walks Uncle James.

Dad has been expecting him. The two men exchange a few words of greeting as Uncle James goes to stand with his back close to the fire, rubbing his hands behind him. He and Dad talk about dogs and about where to hunt coons. Uncle James looks stouter than usual because he is wearing an extra layer of clothes under his overalls. The collar of his red-and-black mackinaw is turned up over the earflaps of his corduroy cap, which are tied under his chin. He and Dad speak the language of coon hunters— a jargon of place names that mean little or nothing to me.

Dad goes out to the back porch and brings the lantern. After checking the kerosene in it, he raises the glass and holds a burning match to the wick. Though saturated with kerosene, the wick is so cold that the match nearly burns his fingers before the yellow flame catches on and broadens across the wick. Dad lowers the glass and adjusts the height of the flame. Soon the smell of burning kerosene and hot metal rises from the lantern.

Time to go. My brother and I put on our jackets and caps and gloves, if we can find them, and follow the men out onto the front porch, where the dogs are jumping around and whining in their eagerness, their toenails clacking and scratching on the wooden porch floor. We have two black-and-tan hounds now, young dogs that Dad got after the death of Blue, now buried with honors under the big walnut tree between the house and the barn.

Uncle James carries the lantern. Dad and my brother take the rifle and axe leaning outside the front door, and we move out into the sharp, cold darkness. In the valley to the east the land has been partly cleared, but elsewhere the woods stretch unbroken for miles over some of the roughest terrain in the world, the Cookson Hills. Almost at once we are in the woods. There is no moon, and the night is calm and cloudless, but there is a high veil of haze, and only a few dim stars glimmer through the tracery of branches overhead.

With nothing to carry, I trudge along behind the others, stumbling over rocks and logs as I dodge the backlash of sprouts and low-hanging limbs of trees. The yellow halo of lantern light reveals the trunks of trees within its small circle and casts drifting shadows that make even familiar spots look strangely different. The first shock of the cold wears off, and the hard walking warms me up. But before we have covered half a mile our constantly changing course through the woods has wiped out my sense of direction.

We cross a stretch of high ground, and now the terrain ahead of us slopes down abruptly to a ledge of gray rock, beyond which the lantern light empties into a dark void. We have come to the edge of the bluff somewhere north and west of our house. Here we stop to regroup. Even Uncle James is not sure exactly where we are, so Dad takes the lantern and leads the way along the rim of lichen-coated bluff rock to a place where we can go down. There is no trail, but Dad is well acquainted with every getting-down place. This one is a kind of steep natural stairway across the

face of the bluff. Most of the steps are missing. Dad goes first
with the lantern, and the light picks up the tops of bare trees below us. He warns us to watch our footing while he holds up the
lantern to light the way over the drop-offs.

The dogs have ranged and fallen behind, but when Dad whis-
tles for them they come plunging down to the bluff's edge, where
they hang back, squirming and whimpering and fearful of the
four- or five-foot steps down the all-but-impossible route Dad has
taken. He orders them to come on, but they fidget and tremble,
their heads low and their paws on the brink of rock, not quite able
to commit themselves to the fearful headlong plunge. Seeing that
they do not obey orders, Dad goes back grumbling and lifts them
down the first big step. After that they cannot retreat and must
follow where he leads. The rocky descent slants down across the
face of the bluff in an unpredictable way, and our pace is slow and
tortuous. As we get lower, the air grows colder, and our creeping
rate slows my blood. My ears and nose are aching with cold. Unable to find my mittens before we left the house, I keep my hands
in my pockets whenever I can.

At the foot of the bluff we flounder through a chaotic jumble of
huge rocks and grapevine and drifts of dead leaves that hide the
treacherous footing of the uneven ground. We make our way onto
more open ground on the slope of the mountainside, where the
trees are enormous and there is less underbrush. The dogs have
gone off on their own now and are out of sight and hearing. We
skid down the flank of a deep ravine with a strip of icy dark water
at the bottom, all clogged with dead leaves, and struggle up the
other side.

A dog barks in the distance—one of ours—so we stop and listen and try to get his bearings. The barking is resumed and now
the other dog joins in. Both dogs are barking fast and furiously.
When I catch up with the men, I can see by the lantern's light that

Dad's face has a doubtful look. The dogs are not on a trail. They are someplace near the foot of the bluff we came down, but farther away. They sound like dogs in a rage, not like dogs barking to call for help.

Dad is not happy. He knows what the dogs have got mixed up with, and it does not raise his opinion of them. He judges all dogs by the measure of Blue, his hunting partner for twelve years, and he has never found Blue's peer. "Skunk," he says. "Probably in the bluff." He gives a shrill commanding whistle and whoops for the dogs, but they ignore him. No doubt they are unable to hear him over their own hysterical outcry.

Our breath fogs in the cold half-darkness as we stand in the woods. My toes are numb, and I shuffle my feet restlessly. But Dad says that if we join the dogs we will only be encouraging them in their foolishness. Before long, however, he concludes that there is no help for it, so we make our way up and across the high ground in the direction of the frantic barking.

We find the two black-and-tan hounds in a lathered frenzy, digging away madly at an excavation under a cabin-size chunk of fallen bluff rock. There is no doubt about a skunk at the bottom of all this. The skunk has been firing wildly, and near the rock the smell is so strong that I gag and retch. There is a terrible difference between the skunk odor that wafts across a road at night and the smell of a skunk fighting for its life at close quarters. There is no describing it except to say that it is unique and awful.

The dogs are out of control and refuse to give up their hopeless siege until cajolery and threats and physical and verbal abuse at last prevail. We take them away in quest of more worthy game. We go down the mountainside and across another ravine and come to a branch of flowing water, where the dogs stop to lap a long time. The smell of skunk clings to them persistently. Dad suspects they have deadened their noses and may be good for nothing the rest of the night. But after drinking their fill they are more calm and seem ready for whatever may befall them. They range on ahead, minding their business.

I have seen nothing familiar for a long time. The trees seem incredibly tall because their tops are lost in darkness, and the background visible through the trunks by day is completely missing. After a long time Dad calls a halt and says we will build a fire and rest and wait to hear from the dogs. He rakes dry leaves out of a narrow space under a rock, breaks up a fistful of dead twigs and small branches, and puts them on the leaves. Then he scrapes a match on a rock and thrusts the spurting flame into the leaves, where it burns steadily and spreads its yellow fire in the heap.

The fire grows quickly as we put on more dry dead branches, and as the flames leap higher a big sycamore tree appears close at hand. It emerges from darkness and looms up to a fantastic height, with its white limbs reflecting the light of the flames. The dim spot where we are sitting has become a place. We are the center of a broad circle of golden firelight ringed by trees. The sound of splashing water comes from nearby, and Dad says we are at the pipe spring near the north end of the mountain. I am surprised and look around at the scene again. I have been here a few times by day, but everything looks different now and mysteriously better somehow.

When I have thawed out my toes and fingers I eat the peanuts that I put in my pocket before leaving home. We linger by the fire until we are thoroughly warm and I am comfortably tired. The peanuts are all gone, and Dad has smoked his pipe out. We have heard nothing from the dogs, but when the fire burns low Dad gets up and stamps out the embers, and off we go again through the deep woods, taking our dim circle of lantern light with us. The feeling of place is lost at once, for the lantern makes only a small hole in the immense darkness.

I am cold and tired and ready to go home, but I know that the least complaint or whine will break the spell that has brought us here. So when Dad asks if I am OK I do my best to sound delighted to be where I am. He tests me, asking if I want to go home, and I manage a firm no, echoing my brother.

I have no idea how long we have been in these woods. I have no idea where we are in relation to anything smaller than the moon. We trudge over endless ridges, through unbroken woods, and down deep hollows where the cold air hangs heavy with the smell of leaf mold and decaying wood. At length the dogs set up a hue and cry half a mile away, but before we can get far in their direction they fall silent again and presently rejoin us, trotting into the lantern light with their tongues hanging to the ground. The smell of skunk lingers about them still, and Dad and my uncle agree that their noses have been so numbed that they could scent a coon only if one stopped them to ask for directions.

We come to a creek with a broad gravel bed and a deep, narrow channel of fast-flowing water. We do not cross the creek but follow its bank downstream to a small tributary branch, which we follow away from the creek for a ways. Then we turn away from the branch and climb a steep, flinty ridge to a flat spot where there is a long-abandoned field overgrown with sprouts and grass. At the edge of the field is all that remains of what was once a house—rough floorboards set on a foundation of flat rocks. We walk across the floor, our heavy shoes clumping loudly, and there is only a little debris of broken glass and dust and accumulated leaves. When Dad says, "I've been to many a dance right here, in this house," I try to imagine what it was like, but my brain is too cold to do much with it.

A little later, to my astonishment, we come to the remains of our former campfire and stop to rebuild the fire and get warm again. My uncle is a tobacco chewer, and he takes out a flat brown cake and cuts off a portion. With his knife point he pries out a small red tin star that is pressed into the tobacco. It falls at his feet and I reach to get it.

We put out the fire once more, and this time when we leave we are headed in what I believe is the way home. But before we have walked a hundred yards we hear the dogs barking again, a long way off. "They're on the other side of the mountain," says my brother, stating what is painfully clear. The dogs have got adrift and roamed so far that they have put between us and them a half mile of the roughest ground in the country.

The dogs are serious this time. Every faraway yelp tells Dad that they have honestly got a coon up a tree. This is the moment when the true coon hunter reveals his colors. No more tired and sleepy. No more dawdling and sightseeing. Dad sets the course and leads the way, lantern in hand, up the leafy, boulder-strewn slope to the bluff, then up the broken face by a different trail just as tortuous as the one we came down. My uncle and my brother and I follow with rifle and axe, busting our knees on rocks, and reach the top of the bluff winded but warm. The others take off at once, but I look back over the valley and see the gray woods stretching unbroken in the distance, and in all that vast expanse there is not a light.

We cross the end of the mountain at a shuffling trot, stumble through a sprout-invaded clearing where the Indians lived, and go into the woods again and down the bluff once more, by a trail even more hazardous. We tear our skin on briars and break our shins on snags and find the dogs on a narrow ridge crest, leaping and yelping around the base of a red oak tree.

I peer up into the tangled branches and can see nothing, but Dad's practiced eye picks out a patch of gray fur. He and my uncle take turns with the axe, and a lengthy spell of hard work brings the tree crashing at an angle into a ravine. Now there is a great uproar with men yelling, dogs yapping, boys whooping, and the coon snarling as he fights free of the fallen tree branches. The rifle is useless in the melee, and the coon, after tangling briefly with one of the dogs and slashing its nose, swiftly eludes his pursuers and streaks for the safety of the bluff at an amazing speed. Then his luck runs out. Before he has gone fifty feet the dogs overtake him and maul him to death before Dad can restrain them. He is concerned to save the coon's skin, not its life. The dogs have been nursing their wrath over the humiliating treatment by the skunk, but Dad drives them away from the carcass and hefts the dead coon by its tail and looks it over. It is not the biggest coon he ever caught, but it is full grown.

Nobody has spoken the word "home," but when we set off again that is where we are going, through territory as strange to me as Poe's Dreamland—a place of chasms and caves and titan woods. At last I see that we are on the steep, twisting single-lane road that struggles up the ravine to our house. We have been wandering through a mysterious realm for ages, it seems, and my brother and I stumble into the house and fall into our bed like small logs.

The next day Dad skins the coon and stretches its pelt with the fur side in, on a tapered board, and hangs it on the wall of the old log house where he used to live but which is now a toolshed. While he is doing this, my uncle turns up again, and they talk over last night's hunt. Uncle James reminds Dad of a time, years ago, when Dad took him hunting and gave him the coonskin to sell for the money to pay for his marriage license. Dad smiles a rare smile, and James chuckles in his soft, reminiscent way. "Never needed another one," he says. "And hope I never do."

17 **1936**

IT SEEMS FITTING, when I look back on it, that 1936 was the year I discovered reality—that is to say, a world without Santa Claus—because it was that kind of year all around. People who can remember five decades still speak of 1936 as the pit of the Great Depression. The drought was dryer, the heat was hotter, jobs were fewer, and money was scarcer. It was the year when the largest number of record-high temperatures was set and the dust bowl overflowed, the year the Joads went to California in their patched-up jalopy. I think of it as the year when we all slept on the front porch—until we too went to California.

It is easy to remember the day we left for California, because it was my seventh birthday. Family birthdays were not ever affairs of state with us, but they usually brought forth a cake from Mother, always eager to please somebody in the kitchen. That year, however, there was no chance to bake anything, and my birthday might have passed unnoticed in the other, more important events of the day. But Mother found another way to make the occasion memorable.

The first gray light of a summer dawn was in the air, and the elm trees in front of Grandma's house were a-twitter with early sparrows. My brother and I crawled into our car and settled comfortably on the quilts stacked in the back seat. We did not go back to sleep, because we knew this was a day that would make a difference. Perched on the stack of quilts, I was in a position to see the world without having to crane my neck, as I usually did. I didn't want to miss anything.

My brother, who was two years older than I, was so caught up in the spirit of going to California that he resolved to keep a notebook record of every town we went through on our trip. And he did. I was going to keep a record too, but I gave it up after the first day. There were too many towns, and in those pre-interstate days the hamlets and villages and cities—even the largest—were strung on the two-lane highways like Indian beads on a string. My brother kept his resolve and noted them all. He is still an authority on this subject and can tell me where we spent the night at every stage of our five-day trek to California.

My own record, such as it is, comes from the floppy disk of memory, which, though incomplete, is accurate as far as it goes. Let's see what views of the past I can call up onto the visual display window.

Here is a good clear picture of the main street of Cleveland, Oklahoma—a little town in the hills northwest of Tulsa somewhere. It is still there, of course, but it has never amounted to much, and in 1936 it was already running on empty—coasting, you might say, on the memory of its brief day of boomtown glory when Tulsa was the oil capital of the world. My father knew all about that, but it meant little to me. What caught my astonished attention was the streets. The main street was an unbroken expanse of red bricks in a pattern, straight up a steep hillside. I had seen stores built of bricks, and even a few houses in Muskogee and Fort Smith. But a whole street of bricks! It seemed to me that Cleveland was far ahead of the rest of the world.

Our car, a new Chevrolet of a dark maroon color, is parked at an angle there on Cleveland's steep street of bricks. Inside the car, stuporous from the hundred-degree heat, my brother and I and Dad are waiting for Mother to come out of the grocery store where she had gone to buy something for our supper. She returns with a sack full of things, from which she takes a small paper bag and passes it back to us. In it are two bunches of grapes, but when we see them our faces fall. They are green! Mother and Dad laugh at our expressions and explain that the grapes are actually ripe. But knowing Mother's penchant for small practical jokes I hold back while my brother takes a tentative bite on one grape. When I see how quickly his expression changes as he takes another one, I am convinced that the grapes are edible and soon prove it for myself. We leave Cleveland, then, considerably less ignorant than when we arrived. Red brick streets and ripe green grapes! What next?

The next scene is late in the same day—our first day on the road—and the time is late in the afternoon, almost sundown. Our car is stopped off the shoulder of the two-lane highway somewhere in western Kansas. There is no traffic on the road and no houses or settlement to be seen. In our family group a picnic mood prevails as Mother spreads a quilt over the dry roadside grass and prepares our supper. She makes sandwiches of cheese or "lunch meat" and fills our cups with water from the thermos jug, which has been refilled with ice at a filling station. She has two surprise treats for us—potato chips to eat with our sandwiches and, in honor of my seventh birthday on this seventh day of August, a ripe watermelon! She has smuggled the watermelon into the car unseen, somehow, and I feel greatly flattered and important. Even now, given the choice between cake and watermelon, I will choose the melon. Of course, some cakes are better than some watermelons, but the best melon surpasses any cake.

So there we are, the four of us, beside the lonely road at sundown, eating our supper on the ground beside the car. The road is lost to sight in the distance, and on either side of it the flat, dry fields stretch away to the horizon. The sun is poised on the western edge of the earth, casting a long red light through the dusty air, and our shadows stretch eastward out of sight.

The next scene is late in the morning of our second day on the road. We are driving west over the longest and straightest road I have ever seen. For hours we have held the same course, varied only by the long, slow rolling of the terrain, which has been rising steadily and almost imperceptibly for four hundred miles. Here there are no fences along the road, for there are no fields, only dry ditches and endless tracts of sage and mesquite and clumps of dead-looking grass whose roots barely manage to hold onto the ground. The sky and sun are brilliantly clear, except for a few puffs of white cumulus far ahead in the west.

My brother and I are sprawled on the stack of quilts in the back seat with the windows down and the dry wind whipping our hair in our eyes. We are alert, however, and for the last thirty miles our attention has been fixed on the horizon ahead of us, where Dad says the Rocky Mountains will soon come into sight. I can see nothing of the mountains yet, and I do not know what they will look like, but I am determined not to miss them.

The mountains, when they appear, are not what I had expected. There is no sudden apocalyptic vision, but a slow coming to realize that what I am seeing is part of the same world over which we have been traveling for a day and a half. First there is a gray line across the west, then a misty blue-gray veil that takes on substance and looks like a great wall. Finally we can perceive diamond-bright streaks and spots of snow flashing along the crest of the range. Our *oohs!* and *aahs!* are blown away by the wind as we look on, and our mouths are parched by the thin, dry air of the high plains east of Denver.

Here now is the city, the heart of downtown Denver as it was in the summer of 1936. It is Sunday, and the streets look strangely empty. It is so clear that you can see for miles along the main street, which was the main east-west highway then, and straight through to the mountains beyond.

There are traffic lights at the intersections, but little traffic, and in the thin, dry air the mountains appear deceptively close. A little way beyond the golden-domed capitol, Dad parks the car at an angle in one of the abundant parking places in the center of town. I go with my mother across the street to a big drug-and-sundries store. While she is buying whatever she came for, I wander around the store looking at things. Most of the things mean nothing to me, but when my eye falls on a wooden model of a twin-engine airplane I am unable to tear myself away. I do not even try to tear myself away.

Airplanes have begun to replace locomotives as the objects of my infatuation. But airplanes are still a novelty to us. When an airplane flew over Coon Mountain—a rare event—we would go out in the yard and shade our eyes from the sun and try to catch sight of it. I have never seen a plane up close or even a realistic picture of one. Fascinated by the model, I stand there trying to memorize every detail of it until Mother takes me firmly by the arm and leads me away. In a trance still, I try to tell her that a wooden model airplane would be a valuable and useful thing for her to buy. The price is only $1.25. I am sure that if I could only express myself clearly she would understand and agree with me. But before I can well begin it is too late. We are out of there and across the street before I can even get started on my plea.

The English mystic William Law believed that man was a stranger on this planet who had wandered out of paradise and, as he put it, fallen captive to the stars and elements. Maybe so.

Now it is late in the afternoon and we are west of Denver. We have spent some time at a zoo, of which I am unable to retrieve any picture, and Dad is trying to make up for what he considers lost time. But fortune does not favor him, for the road is not a good one for making up lost time. When it encounters the mountains it takes a direct, head-on approach up the steep slope, going back and forth in switchback turns. Each mile-long stretch is a ramp on the mountainside that leads up to a hairpin curve and another long, straight stretch. The surface is gravel, and the rear tires spin on the curves and throw rocks out into space behind us.

Though the car is new—a six-cylinder Chevrolet sedan—it is not one of General Motors' greatest triumphs of design. (1936! Everything was lousy that year.) The combination of the load, the heat, the altitude, and the steep grade prove more than the cooling system can handle. The marker of the temperature gauge moves steadily over to the red mark and stays there while Dad scans the mountain with a desperate eye. There is no stopping place; he must push on.

We are high up on the mountain now, and when I look back through the rear window I see the plains spread out maplike far below, with Denver in the hazy distance. It is scary, and I turn to keep my eyes away from the drop-off beside the road. I look at the rugged mountain slope on the near side, bare of trees here.

Dad sits up straight, close to the steering wheel, trying to see the road over the hood, which points skyward into space. His hands are gripping the wheel tightly, and he mutters something when the rear end slides going around a hairpin turn. Beside him, Mother is silent and a bit rigid, with a drawn look on her face. Perhaps she is praying.

At last luck turns in Dad's favor. Near the crest of the mountain ridge we come to a culvert where a small stream flows under the road and there is a clear, flat place where we can pull over and stop. We wait there while the engine cools, and the purple shadow of the mountains stretches out on the eastern plains. Dad removes the radiator cap and pours in water from the stream. After that he has no wish to linger admiring the view. We push on.

We arrive at a tourist court in a small town in the mountains long after dark that night, so I cannot call up a picture of the place. But the air is cool and pine scented, and I can hear the enchanting sound of a mountain stream splashing over rocks in the darkness nearby. My brother and I crawl into a bed and huddle under blankets for the first time in months, and I am asleep at once.

Dad liked to get what he called an early start when he was traveling. To him this meant being on the road before there was any hint of daylight in the sky. In this he was typical of his generation, which carried on the tradition of their forebears who traveled by horse and wagon and had to make the most of the cool, quiet hours before sunrise. Whatever the reason, he liked to have half a day's traveling behind him before he ate breakfast.

This morning was cold, and Dad rousted us from our bed in the darkness. All a-shiver, we dressed and wrapped ourselves in quilts as soon as we were in the car and went back to sleep. When we woke up it was time for breakfast, and we were many miles down the road.

The next scene is a striking contrast to the little mountain town where in my memory it is always night. This picture is like an overexposed snapshot, a blinding glare of dazzle in which details are few. Obviously we are somewhere in the Great Salt Lake Desert of Utah. The sunlight reflected from the crust of minerals is so bright and unrelieved that Dad gives in to Mother's suggestion that he buy himself a pair of sunglasses. He has always looked on sunglasses as self-indulgent finery, but once he gives in the bars are down, and all of us must have sunglasses—which is precisely what he had known would happen.

My brother and I now view the arid wastes of the salt desert through our glass eyes darkly. We are wondering if what we see in such unlimited abundance is indeed salt. There is only one way to find out for sure. When Dad stops at a filling station we venture out onto the edge of the crust. It is dirty and crystalline, with a glazed look, and I suspect that it is bitter. We break off little pieces and look at them closely. They are not inviting to taste, and our tentative experiments are inconclusive.

Two more days and nights we are on the road, creeping across the brown hell of Nevada's empty miles, always within sight of arid, jagged-toothed ranges. At Reno we turn north and west, on the road to Susanville and the High Sierra. During this time my memory apparatus stopped recording the kind of pictures it had taken earlier. But those first impressions have served me well, and I still regard the world as a place of unexpected wonders.

WE RETURNED FROM California in the spring of 1937 and lived for a year in Stilwell, in a shabby old house a couple of blocks north of Main Street. The house, with its sagging porches and windows darkened by overgrown shrubbery, belonged to an eccentric old lady who carried her dead husband's ashes about with her in her purse. But that was her misfortune. We had enough problems of our own, like almost everybody else at that time.

Our family situation was too complicated to explain, but probably not much different from that of any other family struggling to make it through hard times. My brother and I spent the summer days at Grandma Ross's house in the south end of Stilwell. She fixed lunch for us and let us do what we wanted the rest of the time, provided that we stayed out from underfoot. Her house was on a big corner lot with elm trees and a mulberry tree that made a mess of the sidewalk. In the back was an old garage in a state of disrepair, some sheds, a chicken house, and a garden plot. Grandma raised chickens, and in the garden she grew tomatoes, eggplant, rhubarb, and dock weed, among other things.

Her house stood near the edge of town on a corner where two unpaved streets petered out. The lot across the street, in front, was vacant, Across the street on the west side stood the Snodgrass house, a nice big two-story dwelling.

Stilwell had not been planned, it had just happened. Its seventeen hundred or so inhabitants were not burdened with zoning laws and restrictive ordinances. There was a mayor (unpaid) and a volunteer fire department (whose chief was my uncle Rob Worsham), and a constable (paid, but not well paid). People kept whatever livestock they could afford—even guinea hens, noisiest of fowls. Grandma's neighbors kept both cows and chickens.

The Snodgrass place had been a farm, and to a degree still was, having an orchard and some pasture acreage along with the house and barn and other outbuildings. There were a number of children in the family, and though most were years older than my brother and I, we soon made friends with twelve-year-old Eugene Snodgrass, who generously took us as his protégés that summer.

Eugene's name was too refined sounding for Stilwell boys, so everybody except his parents called him Ooky, which was the name we knew him by. He was an interesting boy, always up to something and dragging us along with him. I seldom had a clear idea of what we were doing, but it usually seemed like fun. Ooky was an eager collector of box tops. Cereal boxes all bore a list of things you could get by sending in the specified number of cardboard tops. There was no end of desirable things, from flashlights and cap pistols—which could be had for a paltry few hundred box tops—to bicycles with headlamps that must have been worth a million. Ooky was always on the lookout for box tops and had already collected several dozens of various kinds. I don't remember his ever sending them in to the Battle Creek address, but he was always on the point of doing so. What he wanted to get I can't remember, but it was something so rare and mysteriously wonderful that the mere prospect of it had me in a charm. His personality was such that he could just talk about things and make them seem within reach of our grasping fingers.

One hot afternoon Ooky came out of his house and beckoned to us, where we were sitting in the shade of the elm tree in front of Grandma's house. We joined him eagerly and followed him along the weed-grown alley and down the next street to a filling station three blocks away. It was one of those old country-town stations, the kind with a covered driveway in front and living quarters upstairs. Inside was a grocery with a candy counter

that we were in the habit of visiting when we had a few cents
to spend.

On this day we had no money, and Ooky was not interested in
the candy counter. He hadn't told us what he was up to, but it
turned out that he was going to play the punchboards. The
punchboard he wanted to play was not one that paid money, however, but one with prizes of candy of a kind not available elsewhere and which we had never even seen before—pecan rolls.
There were more than a dozen of them, the largest weighing more
than a pound.

Each punch of the punchboard cost a nickle, and as the board
was practically new, there were dozens of unpunched holes. To
our amazement Ooky laid a ten-dollar bill on the counter and proceeded to punch out every remaining number in the board. As for
the money, well, Ooky collected not only box tops but scrap iron
and aluminum as well, and there was a place in town where you
could sell it. We had scoured the alleys and trash piles for discarded pots and pans. But I knew without having to be told that
Ooky had not sold that much scrap metal. There wasn't ten dollars worth of scrap aluminum in the county.

Punching out the numbers was merely a formality, since Ooky
had bought all of them. He didn't get back much change from
his ten-dollar bill, but he won all the pecan-roll candy in sight.
There was so much that the station proprietor put it in a big brown
paper bag.

We learned later that Ooky had swiped the ten-dollar bill from
his mother's purse. We also learned that he had got a hell of a
whipping for it. But he seemed to feel that on the whole it had
been worth doing. He ate most of the candy himself, I should
add. And that was fair enough, considering the price he paid, although it not doubt hastened the decay of his teeth, which already
needed attention.

Ooky Snodgrass was no exception in the matter I just mentioned. The number of people you saw in those days whose teeth needed attention was an indicator of the shabby state of the country. Stilwell suffered less from the Great Depression than did the rest of the country, because at its most prosperous the standard of living there was far below the national average. Its distinctions were all dubious ones, so I am obviously not boasting when I say that Adair County was first in poverty, first in sickness, first in violence, and first in the proportion of its population with Indian blood.

Indian blood was not the cause of the social ills. But the Cherokee Nation had got on the wrong side of the federal government long ago, and had been stripped of its leaders and institutions by the laws of the Reconstruction days. Forced to adopt a way of life they did not want and which they had no economic means to support, the Cherokees were a demoralized tribe.

Their nation had been divided into districts, one of which was the Flint district. The settlement by that name changed its name to Stilwell when the railroad came through, in honor of the railroad's founder. The railroad did little to promote lasting prosperity, but it kept hope alive and provided a contact with the larger world.

In the 1930s there were many old wooden-faced full-blood Cherokees who spoke only their tribal language. They were nearly all poor and lived on small farms back in the hills. They were recognizably Indian, but they dressed like everybody else and cut their hair short. The majority of Cherokees were of mixed ancestry and mostly identified as whites. Appearance was no guide to race. Anyone with a full-blood grandparent was listed as Indian on the rolls; less than a fourth meant you were not Indian for all practical purposes.

The prominent Cherokee leader John Ross was himself only about one-eighth Indian, genetically speaking. Sometimes people ask me, in a polite way, if I am one of John Ross's descendants.

The truth is that I have often wondered that myself. John Ross came from a very large and prolific family, and his own children were so numerous that his descendants must now number in the thousands. So the question is all but irrelevant. My father never claimed to have any Cherokee blood, and he refused to identify with them openly. "They lost their land back East," he would say. "Then they came west and lost their land out here." He would go on like that, but in his heart he loved the old way of life and followed it as much as he could. His family had lived among the Cherokees in Georgia and had come west with them—probably before the removal. If so, they were among the "Old Settlers," many of whom opposed Chief Ross later, which would explain their reluctance to dig up the past. But I want to make a final point: the whole idea of deriving status or reflected glory from a family tree is not an American Indian concept. It obviously comes from Europe, where it has long been deeply ingrained. But with the exception perhaps of the Aztec and Inca dynasties—which I do not regard as typical of Native American culture—the rule in force has always been to refrain from claiming kin to the dead.

One of my father's sisters married a Cherokee, as did two of my mother's sisters. So, although I have always been a *yo-nay,* or white man, I had three uncles on the tribal roll, and of course numerous cousins. Little was made of this, and none of my cousins learned to speak the Cherokee tongue. In a way that is a loss. But, although it is among the most beautiful of languages, Cherokee has only a limited survival value in the mainstream world culture now in the making.

Back in the weed-grown, sultry summer of 1937, we roamed the alleys and searched for boxtops and scrap metal until the beginning of the school year put an end to our carefree existence. School was bed news for me again that year. I was in the fourth grade, but in my three years in school I had not learned much except how to read. In arithmetic I had learned to add and subtract, but now I was supposed already to know the multiplication table, which was taught in the third grade in the Stilwell school. I was confronted with the disgraceful prospect of being demoted and, seized with anxiety, I worked on the multiplication table as a matter of life or death. My teacher, Miss Alyne, was too close a friend of my family to have ever ejected me from her class without Mother's consent, but she was an energetic and competent teacher who believed in motivation by anxiety or any other means that worked. She kept her twenty-five or thirty pupils well in hand.

I learned the multiplication table. Then I found that I was not as good a reader as I thought. My report card for that year has survived—though I can't imagine why anybody wanted to keep it—and shows that I had no obvious talent in anything. Art, Music, and Health—C; Arithmetic—C+(!); Reading—B. The only A on the card is for spelling.

I have said that Miss Alyne believed in motivating her pupils, and I think she was better with a carrot than a stick. Those of us who learned our weekly spelling list well enough to spell the twenty-five words correctly were rewarded with more than a good mark. The test was given at the end of the day on Friday afternoons. We exchanged papers and graded them, and those who had made no errors were allowed to leave the second-floor classroom by way of the tubular fire-escape exit at the back of the room. We had to wait until the bell rang, but even before it had stopped clanging the first of the fourth grade's perfect spellers had zoomed down the slippery tube and shot forth to hit the gravel running. Miss Alyne knew the hearts of fourth-graders. She trained a generation of outstanding spellers before the school burned down one summer and was replaced by a modern one-story structure.

Those were brief moments of brightness in an otherwise dreary year. A stranger looking at the children playing on the Stilwell school ground then would have been struck by their clothing. About half the children dressed exactly alike, in corduroy jackets and corduroy pants or skirt—all of them maroon or dark blue. These were provided by the federal government through a New Deal agency. There was also a free lunch program, but the food was reputed to be not good and to consist of many beans and much salt pork.

I never liked school. This is no reflection on the Stilwell school or on any of the schools I attended, or on any of my teachers. I wouldn't have liked *any* school. I learned to endure it, however, and when I was of an age when it was no longer compulsory I grew to enjoy most of my classes. To me a university represents the ideal society.

Be that as it may, I made it through the fourth grade, and when spring came fate smiled on me again. I was free not only from the classroom but from the gloomy old house in town as well. We moved back to our house on Coon Mountain, to the airy spaciousness of it and the smell of honeysuckle in the yellow lamplight and the loud chiming silence of the dark.

19 THE NEWS

SOMETIMES I HEAR people complain that "the news" is depressing because it is always bad. I sympathize with them, but I want to say this: if you think the news is bad these days, you should have heard it in the years between 1938 and 1942. That was about the time I first became aware that there was something called the news.

Dad was one of the few in our community who took a daily newspaper. He subscribed to *The Muskogee Phoenix,* which came by mail. About 1939 he bought a battery-powered radio—the kind with a fifteen-pound dry-cell battery—so he could listen to the news. He liked to know what was going on in the world, though it never seemed to make any difference on Coon Mountain.

I soon grew to hate the news and the grim tones of the voices that brought it to our living room. I tried to pay no attention to it, but I couldn't escape the voices and the sobering effect they had on the grown-ups.

But as much as I tried not to admit it, I knew that the sky was falling. Looking back, it seems as if the war was always coming toward us, as indeed it was. But the beginning of it, the invasion of Poland in 1939, passed without my noticing it—probably because Poland meant nothing to me; I didn't even know what it was, much less where. And I think it may have fallen before we had a radio. But the next year, with Dad and Grandma and Mother listening to the news every day, I couldn't help knowing there was big trouble in England.

There was never any question of whose side to be on. Even Dad, who tended to be contrary and opinionated, took up for the

British, despite an anti-English bias that had been reinforced by his contacts with the English in their colonial role in Latin America. The total lack of pro-German feeling in our part of the country corresponded to the complete absence of Germans or German Americans.

The songs of England were popular on the radio that year. "The White Cliffs of Dover" and "The Shrine of Saint Cecilia" threw an aura of religious sentiment over Britain in its finest hour. I incorporated the blitz into my games and sent flights of toy Stukas and Spitfires into combat. I liked the songs and began to find the news about the war tolerably interesting. I assumed it would remain in England.

Next year the blitz tapered off and the news was nothing but dreariness again. The only bright spot—and it brought a spark of interest to me—was the summer morning when I heard Dad and his friends discuss the news that Hitler had invaded Russia. Their tone of voice was so noticeably different that my ears pricked up. I could sense relief and satisfaction. They were sure that Hitler had blundered at last and would come to grief. Their view proved right in the long run, of course, but in the months that followed many reversed their first opinion. The Red Army collapsed again and again, and Hitler looked more unstoppable than ever.

I lost patience with the war at that stage for a long time. The news was no fun at all. I wanted nothing to do with it. After all, the news was on for only fifteen minutes at a time, once or twice a day, and I could do my chores or other business during that time.

We came to rely on the radio for company and entertainment, and most of the power in its big dry-cell battery was expended on material less weighty than the Gabriel Heater show. As the battery power waned, the speaker volume grew fainter and fainter until it could no longer be heard by the human ear. It could still be heard, however, by my brother when a Cardinals baseball game was on the air. He would sit for hours crouched with his ear pressed to the speaker louvers, like one in a trance. Nobody else could hear a thing.

His mind was affected by baseball. A few times I was wakened in the night by my brother's voice and discovered that he was listening to a baseball game in his sleep, with his head against his pillow. He would mutter the names of players, and when I asked him the score he would reply with rational numbers. When I told him about this, he claimed not to believe me. He got even with me later by swearing me to secrecy and confiding that he had everything fixed up to run away from home and be a batboy for the Cardinals. This was so farfetched, so unlike my brother, that I believed him. He had never been given to imaginative flights of fancy, but when I questioned him about the details he had the answers at the tip of his tongue. He kept me wondering and half worried for a long time. I wouldn't have given him away, if that was what he wanted, but I hated to think of doing all the chores by myself.

We listened to the juvenile programs—"Jack Armstrong" and "Little Orphan Annie"—and Grandma indulged in the first-edition soaps, in their original, fifteen-minute format. Their names were legion and come readily to mind: "Ma Perkins," "Stella Dallas," "Widder Brown," "Judy and Jane," and "John's Other Wife"—all pretty heavy stuff, mostly morning shows. In the afternoon the fare was lighter and included the delightful "Lorenzo Jones and his wife, Belle," and the unforgettably wacky "Vic and Sade," whose humor was worth cultivating an ear for.

"One Man's Family" was a popular evening show that ran for years as a sort of counterirritant to "Amos and Andy." We did not listen to it. It was a bit too upper middle class for us. The Barber family's problems were not very real by our standards. It was too starchy for me, in any case, though I was not at all discriminating in my tastes. I mention it because its musical theme was unforgettable, and the show was so popular that you could hear its haunting strains everywhere.

The cast of that show included three men who were also the stars of a fifteen-minute adventure serial called "I Love a Mystery," which my brother and I listened to avidly. The three stars' fictional names were Jack, Doc, and Reggie. Each character, who had to be recognizable immediately by his voice alone, was a type, of course, even a stereotype. Reggie was British, and his speech was like David Niven's, the kind of speech Americans recognize as the hallmark of aristocratic superiority. His companion Doc spoke in a deliberately soft, drawling way that was vaguely East Texas—a bit nasal but not unpleasant, though a bit more inflected than true Texas speech. The third adventurer was the leader, Jack, whose speech was free of all regional quirks. Jack could have come from anywhere south of Canada and north of the Rio Grande.

The popular family shows that aired on weekends have been recirculated and reevaluated for years now. They not only entertained us but educated us and held up a mirror to us to show us what we were like. I will mention only one name from that era's list of stars, one that has slipped into permanent eclipse and whose tapes have never been reissued, to my knowledge. Bob Burns, a local celebrity who was a national star for only a year or two, was a homespun humorist from Figure Five, Arkansas, who tried to fill the vacancy left by the death of Will Rogers. But just as he was called up to the big leagues, the national sense of humor took a sharp turn to the right, and Will Rogers's low-key, country-boy humor, which had extended Mark Twain's frontier style into the twentieth century, was displaced almost overnight by the fast-talking, wise-cracking city slicker with a markedly urban, gum-chewing sophistication. The Arkansas drawl of Bob Burns was lost in the crowd noise, but in his time at bat he gave us the word *bazooka*—not for a weapon, but for a musical instrument made of a tin funnel and piece of pipe.

When the chores were all done and the supper dishes washed and dried and put away on Sunday evening, we all settled down in the front room and listened to Jack Benny and the Charlie McCarthy show. We didn't realize it of course, but little by little we were being seduced into the mainstream—as for me, I was dragged in by my funny bone. If I was free before supper on Sundays, I listened to "Gene Autry's Melody Ranch," whose theme song still has nostalgic charm for me, evoking the last days of childhood, which were slipping away with the onset of adolescence and the incessant and unstoppable tide of news.

One gray winter Sunday my brother and I and Robert Meadows walked over the crest of Coon Mountain and went down the bluff and through the leafless woods to the Galcatchers' house, on an errand having to do with a dog. Whose dog we were looking for, and why, or whether we found it—all such matters were erased from my memory by something that happened on our way home.

It was a cold day with a threat of snow in the air. As we were returning homeward late in the afternoon, we encountered Dad, who told us that the Japanese had attacked our navy at Pearl Harbor and the United States was going to be in the war.

I was twelve years old, and while I had almost no idea of what the war would be like, I had the feeling that the world I knew would not survive it. It did not occur to me that I would have to bear arms. My brother, who was fourteen, could only wonder about his chances of being in the war. You could enlist at sixteen, and at eighteen you had to go.

When Robert Meadows heard the news from Dad, he must have felt more shock than he cared to tell about. He was sixteen, and he must have suddenly seen his future go out of control. He got a handle on it, however, and would wait until he graduated from high school before joining the navy. He was later a medic on the cruiser *Atlanta* in the South Pacific—a point worth noting by old navy hands.

That grim Sunday was followed by days of mild, sunny weather. The disaster at Pearl Harbor had no close sequel and no direct consequences for me, so I clung to my childhood, and as Christmas approached I avoided all thought of the war. Luckily for me Christmas was in place when the war started. It was the last of my childhood.

We had raised a profitable crop of peaches that year, and I hoped for a lot of presents. My parents may have foreseen what the years ahead would be like and made the most of the occasion. I got a chemistry set bigger and better than I hoped for, and a model of the schooner *Bluenose* with a carved pine hull. On a trip to Muskogee, Dad had seen me looking at a toy steam engine in the window of an OTASCO store and asked me if I would like to have it. Naturally I said yes. It was the first time—maybe the only time—he ever deliberately invoked my covetous nature, and I was not about to pass up the chance. He bought the steam engine, and when I opened my gifts on Christmas Eve, I had little left to wish for.

Lost in the spirit of childhood still, I shut out the low, sober voices of the radio news announcing the fall of the British Empire and other unpleasant matters.

The summer of 1942 brought a resurgence of the rapturous exultation in freedom that came at the end of the school year. I fled from the anxieties and complexities of school and the world news into the woods and fields of summer. I had suddenly become aware of the beauty of nature and discovered anew the familiar scenes where I was raised. I felt as if I was seeing it all for the first time—the cliffs and woods and streams, the patches of corn in the creek bottoms, the orchards and the fields of wheat and oats, the barns and houses—all these things were beautiful and good.

Most of that could be traced to puberty, but the effect was heightened and made poignant by the knowledge of the war and the threat it posed for us, or at least to our way of life. As the summer waned I sensed that, though there had been no decision by my parents as yet, our days on the mountain were numbered. This would be our last summer there. And I was homesick for the place even before I left it.

I knew there was too much going on in the world for Dad to be satisfied where we were. He had been too young for the first World War and now he was too old for the second one. But he grew restless. And while I could understand this, I had grown attached to Coon Mountain—just as he had in his own boyhood—and I wanted to stay there.

What I really wanted, deep inside, was for everything to stay as it was, unchanged forever. I wanted Dad to be always strong and firm, my brother always a little ahead of me, my mother and Grandma always cheerful busy around the house—Mother pretty and always young, and Grandma always old but no older than she was. And me always the youngest child, too young to be put into harness. For that I would have been willing to spend nine months of the year in bondage at school, if I could have three months of summer freedom.

The awareness that none of this was to be, and that nothing was going to be the same again, threw a kind of rapturous sadness over our last weeks on Coon Mountain. As my brother and I pushed our bikes up the steep road home after an afternoon in the Echota swimming hole or at Horn Branch, it would come to me with a sudden pang of anguish that I wouldn't always have my brother around, and I would experience a rush of feeling that I had no way to deal with.

In October of that year we moved to town and lived in Grandma's house there. I had cousins living nearby, and I got along well with them, and life went on. But I was homesick for a long time and an aching sense of loss lingered for months.

I hadn't accepted the fact that we were leaving until the last day. When I realized that we wouldn't be spending the night there, I sat on the flagstone steps by the front gate and cried for a long time. Dad came and sat beside me and put his hand on my shoulder. I don't remember what he said, but I got the impression he understood how I felt.

After that I didn't cry any more, but the sickness for home was a fever in me. At Grandma's house in town my spirits drooped. Desperately seeking some relief for the heartache I felt, I ransacked the old Victrola record cabinet in Grandma's living room, where I found some ancient quarter-inch-thick records with songs from the 1920s that expressed a gaiety that was far from what I felt.

Nothing shows more clearly how out of tune I was with the times and the place than the words of this long-forgotten song:

Say it with a ukelele
Play it with a rhythm light and gay!
Say it with a wicked ukelele
If you want to steal a flapper's heart away.

I didn't know what a flapper was and had probably never seen or heard a ukelele, but the song eased my heart. And even more in keeping with the sad mood of those far-off days were the strains of "Marcheta" sung by a tenor of the Rudy Vallee school and sounding faint and far away, as if coming from the distant lost times:

Marcheta . . . Marcheta
I still hear you calling me back to your arms once again

I still feel the spell of your last kiss upon me
Since then life has all been in vain.

And so, in that droopy and dreamy adolescent way that parents find so irritating, I clung to the past and the memory of my childhood home, until the strains of the old songs were drowned by the thunder from Stalingrad and Guadalcanal, and I awoke at last to the news, in this other world.

20 MY UNCLE'S STORE

WHEN I WAS IN high school I worked after school and on Saturdays in my Uncle Rob Worsham's grocery store in Stilwell. It was in the middle of our block-long main street, between a drugstore and a second-hand clothing store. The sidewalk in front was sheltered by a wooden awning supported by posts along the curb. There were no parking meters, and a few old-timers still hitched their saddle horses to the posts out front. But wagons and teams of horses or mules were no longer allowed to park on the main street and had to stand in the alleys. On Saturdays the alley behind my uncle's store was crowded with wagons and teams.

The store was long and narrow, with a heavy front door of wood and glass reinforced with iron bars. In summer the door was propped open to let the air circulate. To keep out the flies there was a screen door with the logo of a bakery worked into the screen wire like needlepoint. The door was recessed into the narrow storefront, leaving a space on each side for a window display. In one hung a bunch of bananas and in the other stood a vegetable rack the like of which I have never seen elsewhere. It was of galvanized tin and shaped like a plump Christmas tree, with half-a-dozen round trays of decreasing size revolving around an upright iron pipe in the center. The pipe took water to the top, where it sprayed out through a nozzle and rained down in a mist over the trays full of cabbage and carrots and beets and turnips. The water that didn't evaporate collected in the trays and trickled down to the bottom tier, where it sometimes overflowed.

Refrigeration was still a luxury, and a home kitchen type of refrigerator sufficed for my uncle's store. In it he kept such things as cottage cheese and sandwich meat, along with whatever fresh beef and pork he had on hand. An old lead-lined pop cooler with sliding doors on top and no refrigeration coils stood broadside to the door up front. Part of my job was to keep it stocked with five-cent bottles of Coke and Dr. Pepper, Orange, Grapette, Nehi, and Cream Soda. The bottles stood neck deep in icy water, and my hands would get numb groping for the bottles that had fallen over. One end of the cooler was reserved for milk, in glass quart bottles with push-in cardboard lids. The milk was not homogenized, so the cream rose in the necks. It was well worth its price, however, of ten cents a quart. Small towns were not zoned then—as many still are not—and people living close to Main Street, as did my uncle, kept cows and chickens. My uncle had three or four cows, which he milked himself and which were driven to and from the pasture a couple of blocks away by my cousins.

I was familiar with the store long before I worked in it. When I was a small child it seemed so vast a place, with so many people and things in it, that I could never comprehend it as a whole. I could make my way through the Saturday throng of customers to the aisle behind the candy counter—a fingerproof structure of oak and glass—where I wasn't supposed to be. The aisle went back past the cash register to a cul de sac, where it ended at a barricade higher than a man's head. Here was the spot where my aunt had her post of duty. She spent much of the day here. Much of her life, in fact, was spent here behind an oak counter so solid and heavy that an earthquake could hardly have shifted it on the concrete floor. The countertop was worn shiny smooth by the countless dimes and nickels and quarters that had passed over it, and from the innumerable packages of beans and other staples that had rested briefly there in transit. Under the countertop were built-in drawers and bins that swung out and down on pivots at the bottom.

The bins held a bushel of beans each. One was full of white

pea-size navy beans, so cool and clean and shiny that you wanted
to plunge your hands into them. Another held the coarser, and to
me less appealing, brown-and-white speckled pinto beans. The
other bins held flat limas, dark kidney beans, and the popular
black-eyed peas. All these were sold by the pound, measured out
in scoopfuls into a tray that hung from the beam scale over the
counter. The same scale was used in weighing out the thick white
slabs of salt pork kept in a wire cage at the end of the counter.

In this corner of the store the air was rich and fragrant, not only
from the beans and salt pork, but from the bulk spices kept in
small drawers—nutmeg, cloves, sage, dill, pepper, tea, sassafras
root, and garden seeds. These too were sold in carefully weighed-
out amounts and poured into small brown paper bags, which were
then rolled neatly down from the top and secured with two turns
of white string tied by hand. The string came from a giant spool
mounted in an out-of-the-way spot high overhead and threaded in
guides to a point directly above the counter, where it hung down
within reach. This was convenient, since you never had to ask
anybody where the string was. But it dangled in the air between
you and the customer and took some time to get used to.

Most fragrant of all was the aroma from the bin of coffee beans
under the grinder. Running the electric coffee grinder and packaging the ground beans was part of a storekeeper's job. My uncle
liked to do it, so I seldom got a chance to grind coffee. When I
did, I enjoyed it. The fumes from the coffee grinder may have
been intoxicating. I have often wondered how anything as bitter
as a coffee bean could have such a delicious smell.

To go any farther into the depths of the store, you had to back
up and slip through the narrow gap between the counter and the
cash register. This led you into the central hub of the store, where
customers circulated around a big potbellied stove. The stove was
the type you would hope to find in a railroad depot in North Da-
kota, if you were trapped in a blizzard. It had once had a coat of

aluminum paint, but that had mostly burned off. Its quarter-inch-thick iron belly was marked by a long horizontal crack, but it was as efficient as ever, and my uncle never hesitated to pour in great scuttlesful of coal. On winter mornings, stoked to its limit, it glowed cherry red, and at full power it positively quivered with heat, becoming in places almost white hot.

By the time my uncle unlocked the front door at seven o'clock on a raw winter morning, the stove would already be roaring with a glowing red spot or two. Soon the first regulars would arrive to take their places on the old seat-polished bench near the stove. All day long a circle of men and women would stand around it, talking a little, but mainly just roasting their faces and fingers.

In those pre-supermarket days a store was not just a place to buy things. It was a meeting place and a place of shelter, a temporary home. By the middle of morning on Saturday, people would be arriving from farms ten miles back in the hills, half frozen after a three-hour wagon ride. They needed a place to thaw out and recuperate before they transacted any business. They didn't spend money every day of the week, and when they did it called for a bit of ceremony and deliberation.

Beyond the stove, toward the rear of the store, you entered a dim, mysterious region where there were seldom any people. An aisle wide enough for just one person at a time led back into the gloom. On one hand rose a mountain range of sacks of flour and bran and chicken feed—all of it in hundred-pound sacks that, if called upon to move, I had to wrestle onto a steel-wheeled dolly, but which my uncle could toss up onto his shoulder with ease.

A stack of forty-pound cubes of stock salt glistened yellow and white. On the other side of the narrow aisle were cartons of canned goods piled in high columns, along with boxes of Baby Ruths and Paydays and other nonperishable things. Wooden cases for empty pop bottles had a place near the back door, where a little light came through the grimy barred windows.

In summer the back door stood open, and you could look out into the alley where the wagons and horses were standing. If it was midday, people would be sitting on the wagon seats or in the wagon beds eating sausage and biscuits out of shiny buckets that had once held ten pounds of lard or a gallon of molasses. A few splurged on a bottle of pop and fifteen cents' worth of cheese and crackers, which they could eat inside if they wanted to. If you were really hungry, my uncle would fix you a generous ham sandwich for a dime, or a baloney sandwich for a nickel.

Away back in the farthest corner, behind the pile of sacks of feed, three big barrels stood upright. One was of steel and held kerosene. It was fitted with a steel pump on top, and you could fill a gallon jug with kerosene with one turn of the pump handle. The next barrel was a wooden one containing vinegar. Its pump was a primitive wooden device with a plunger that you had to lift straight up by grasping a knob shaped like a miniature football. The plunger did not fit tightly, and you were apt to spill some vinegar every time you filled a jug. Not surprisingly, that corner of the store reeked of vinegar and kerosene. The third barrel, which was a steel drum with the top cut out, held the compound of oil and sawdust that we sprinkled on the floor every night before sweeping out.

My cousin remembers another barrel that stood up front near the bread rack and held cookies, which were sold in bulk quantities. But it was gone by the time I worked there, and I am sorry to say that I missed it. But all who can remember the store will recall the five-gallon bottle of Coca-Cola that stood on top of the refrigerator for years. It was a precise replica of an ordinary Coke bottle, and we speculated endlessly as to whether it contained the real thing or only Coke-colored water. Nobody ever dared to suggest opening it to find out. That would have seemed sacrilegious.

My uncle liked to stock as many things as he could besides

groceries. Brooms swung in a wire circle, suspended from the ceiling, and you would come across clusters of brown work gloves, clumps of overalls, traps, canning jars, knives, and minnow buckets. You might find anything in the odd corners.

In another of the out-of-the-way nooks, near the stove but separated from it by a high glass-and-wood display case containing school supplies and God knows what else, was my uncle's office space. His desk was of oak, naturally, and of ample size, with a roll top and numerous pigeonholes. Beside it squatted a massive safe. I say it was massive, but allowing for the enhancement of objects by memory I suppose it weighed less than a heavy cruiser. In it my uncle put each day's cash receipts, this being at a time before banks were accommodating in their hours of deposit. Once the store was burglarized—this was before I worked there—and thieves hauled away my uncle's safe. It was found a few days later near a country road back in the hills, empty of its cash. It was returned to my uncle, who had it worked on and kept using it as before. The thieves were never caught. They must have been strong and desperate men.

For all its apparent lack of organization, the store was efficient. Every foot of floor and wall space was put to use, and only the ceiling was mostly bare. The ceiling was of metal, tin I suppose, stamped with a design of squares in an old-fashioned, unpretentious style. From it hung a series of naked light bulbs that gave the place a bleak look on dark winter evenings, and two or three broad-bladed ventilator fans. The walls were lined with shelves of canned goods, and to get a can of peaches or anything else from the top shelf was a feat requiring some skill. You took a broomstick with a nail driven into it near the end and, after climbing as high as you could, hooked the nail head over the rim of the topmost can. With a quick tug you could topple the can from its place, and if you knew what was good for you, you dropped the broomstick and caught the can before it snapped your collarbone or crushed your foot in its descent. To let a can hit the floor was to disgrace yourself.

The store had not always so well stocked. I have been told that in the worst of the depression its stock was inventoried at less than a hundred dollars. But by patient endurance and a determination to see it through, my uncle and aunt and their store survived and prospered, and within a few years after its lowest ebb it had resurged to the state I have described, with all its space in use.

The sign in front said WORSHAM'S CASH GROCERY. But that expressed an early, idealistic optimism on my uncle's part. Perhaps half of his customers paid cash at the time of purchase. The rest bought their groceries on credit and paid more or less regularly. There was no billing system worthy of the name. A handwritten sales slip for the purchases on credit went into the customer's bag, and a carbon copy was put in the file. I call it a file because I don't know what else to call the device that stood beside the cash register. It was a kind of book, with metal pages hinged at the spine. Each of the metal pages had rows of wire clips, like mousetraps, that held the yellow sales slips in place. The slips accumulated in the specific mousetrap clip assigned to a customer until the bill was paid. I believe they were in alphabetical order by the customer's last names, but I'm not sure.

Clerks were expected to know the customers by name, and the system on the whole left plenty of chances for mistakes by adolescent clerks like me. But my uncle had a good memory and a good disposition. He knew his customers well, and he knew his business, and his system worked well for him. I don't know how regularly or irregularly his debtors paid him. That was never discussed in my presence.

My uncle did not have to practice honesty because it was the best policy. Honesty came as naturally to him as eating and breathing, and he expected it in others. That is, without making a big issue of it he expected people to deal with him honestly. He was not a man to squeeze a nickel, but he had a healthy aversion to being imposed upon or taken advantage of. His judgment was accepted and recognized as good. Most of his customers were poor, and in his long tenure as a storekeeper he must have encountered every aspect of human despair and every degree of shiftlessness. He was a good, kind man, but he can hardly have had any illusions about people.

I have not finished with my uncle's store. The things I have written about were the stage and the stage properties. The essence of the store was people, its customers. And of these a large number were Cherokees. My uncle, though not a Cherokee himself, had learned the Cherokee language and understood the Cherokee ways. His strong identification with his customers, along with his good humor and robust spirit, won him many friends who remained loyal to him over the years.

21 PICKING THINGS

ALMOST EVERYTHING that grows is picked by machines now, which is the way nature meant them to be picked. Throughout most of recorded history, human beings were used as pickers, but the results were seldom satisfactory, at least as far as the picker was concerned. Any work that puts people into close contact with mother earth is going to be laborious, monotonous, and unprofitable, to a degree depending on the closeness of contact. Anthropologists tell us that war itself was invented by men who would rather fight than pick.

I am no mere theorist on the subject. My career as a picker began with strawberries, when I was eleven, and ended four years later when I realized I wasn't getting ahead. I hadn't put as much as a dime aside for my old age. It wasn't my fault: I was as greedy as the next boy, but the much-vaunted rewards of greed weren't coming my way.

I had a clear goal in mind when I started picking. I wanted to earn $4.98 so I could order a miniature gasoline engine kit advertised in *Mechanix Illustrated*. And though I kept my eye on that goal through two seasons of strawberry picking, I never got all those dollars and cents together at the same time.

Anybody could pick strawberries. There were no formalities, not even an official starting or quitting time. Word would get around that a farmer needed pickers on a certain day, and when the day came pickers straggled out of the woods and went to work. You didn't have to tell anybody your name or social security number, you just took one of the wooden trays that held empty quart boxes and started picking. The biggest trays held twelve quarts; they were for serious pickers who could go half a day without water. I used a six-quart tray.

Strawberries, as you know, do not grow on trees or bushes, where they can be seen and easily reached. They grow close to the ground in rocky soil, amid a mass of leaves and tendrils and weeds and grass. Nature hides the best berries, so you have to push aside the leaves and weeds to make sure you are not missing any. This leafy mass is three or four feet wide and extends the length of the field. The picker works between two rows, picking on both sides as he inches along. The field is drenched with dew in the first part of the day. The older the field, the weedier and wetter it will be.

The pickers where I worked made a point of filling their boxes to overflowing, piling on berries till not one more could be added to the heaped-up container. I never understood why they did this; some of the berries always fell off while they were carrying the tray to the shed. And nobody would have rejected a box that was not overflowing.

When all the boxes in your tray were full, you carried them to the shed at the edge of the field, where the farmer or his wife paid you on the spot, five cents a quart. After getting your money, you could quit if you wanted to, and nobody would think worse of you. People didn't pick berries to prove anything. But if you needed more than thirty cents, for any reason, you helped yourself to a dipperful of water from the bucket, took another tray full of empty boxes, and went back to picking.

Until now, we will assume, you have been working in a squatting posture, duck-walking along between the rows to avoid the cold, wet grass and ground. But the muscles in your legs are trembling, and since the dew has dried somewhat you plop on your knees and work that way for a while. Soon an unpleasant dampness seeps through the knees of your overalls where your weight rests, but you get used to that. After stumping along this way for half an hour, the skin on your knees grows sensitive to pressure. Then, as you lurch forward, lugging your tray behind you, your knee comes down on the knifelike edge of a chunk of flint half-buried and hidden under the leaves. Unstrung by the sudden pain, you are unable to keep your balance and tumble face down in the weedy wetness.

You have been working for a couple of hours. If little things do not discourage you, you may work all day. It will not be any easier in the afternoon. The field will be drier, but the sun will be hotter. If the picking lasts much later than one o'clock, the older boys and girls will stop their sly throwing of berries at one another.

If you are lucky, the sky turns gray, and clouds bring relief from the sun. If your luck holds out, the clouds thicken and the sky grows darker. You hear thunder rumbling and growling. A sense of urgency sweeps down the rows, and everyone picks fast in the hope of filling his tray before the storm breaks. A sudden fresh gust of wind carries the smell of rain, then a stronger blast comes bearing scattered stray drops of windblown moisture. A bold of lightning rips at a dead tree at the edge of the field, and you decide to turn in your berries and hurry back to the shed with the thunder crashing about your ears. When you have pocketed your coins, the first sheets of rain drive in the diehard pickers, who come running between the rows with subdued whoops, holding their trays out awkwardly at their sides. Only the farmer will be sorry to see the workday end. Among the pickers a mood of exhilaration prevails.

Pickers were not insured. If you got struck by lightning in the strawberry fields you had only yourself and God to blame. One fringe benefit, aside from the general healthiness of the work, was the opportunity to eat as many berries as you could. This was also true of peaches, which taste even better than strawberries if you catch one at the right moment of perfection. But peaches get

ripe in midsummer, and while the humid heat of the peach orchard is a paradise for wasps and gnats and bees and yellow jackets, it is oppressive to people.

The peach picker has much to endure. He wears a canvas harness strapped about his chest, to which he hooks a canvas sack
that sags below his knees. As the sack gets full of peaches the
picker waddles around, bent over at the hips, until he can find a
basket to empty the peaches into by unhooking the bottom of
the sack.

In the depths of the orchard the summer air is golden with peach
fuzz. It collects under the picker's chin and coats his sweaty body
inside his clothes where the harness rubs. Most of him itches or
stings or burns, and he is like a small child—always thirsty. He is
encumbered not only by his sack and harness but also by his ladder, which he must move from tree to tree, staggering to keep his
balance. Often, when he extends his hand toward a remote high
peach, the limb supporting the ladder yields, the ladder slithers
sideways, and he plunges into leafy space with a cry of despair.

Apple picking was much the same. If it was less uncomfort-
able, it was because the weather in apple time was less humid and
not so invariably hot. The pay was comparable to peach picking:
15¢ an hour. During the Second World War, when there was full
employment and anybody over sixteen could work in a defense
plant for $1.25 an hour, apple pickers were paid $3 a day, which
is about 37¢ an hour.

I have also picked tomatoes for wages, and green beans as
well, and the most I can say for those vegetables is that they are
less fun than peaches and no more profitable to pick. Tomatoes
are heavy and wear you out, while beans are just plain boring.
Worse than any of these, for the picker—the worst of anything
that grows on earth—is okra. Picking okra is like going to war.
Once you have done it, you wonder how they can find people
willing to do it for any amount of money.

I was too young to have any other experience to compare with what I was doing. All pickers complained, in the idle way that soldiers or office workers do. It is a way of keeping a grip on reality. But one autumn day, when I had three or four years' picking experience behind me, something happened that jarred me into giving some thought to the matter and led me to conclude that I was in the wrong field.

It was 1943. We were living in a big sprawling housing area which the government had built for the workers in the Vancouver shipyards. I was fourteen and in the tenth grade at the housing area's junior high school. One foggy morning before school, word came from the principal's office that students who wanted to pick filberts that day would be excused from their classes. This was put to us somehow as part of the great national war effort (a decent-sounding phrase that, like "national security," has cloaked many a selfish act). I volunteered, along with a dozen others, not from any patriotic motive but to break the monotony of school. (I may have been empty-headed, but I wasn't sappy enough the think that picking filberts had anything to do with winning the war.) I also had another motive—greed. I nursed the sneaky hope that as an experienced picker I might make a killing. If they were so badly in need of pickers, I reasoned, they must be paying good wages. It would have been just as logical to reason the other way and come to the opposite conclusion. But greed had warped my judgment.

We got aboard a bus and rode out to the filbert orchard, miles away. There was no shed or office in sight and nobody to tell us what to do. There were some sacks lying around, apparently for pickers, so we took a sack apiece and went to gathering filberts.

Until that day I had never seen a filbert except in a bag of mixed nuts and had no idea where they came from or how they were picked. I soon learned that they grow on gnarled trees whose branches hang low to the ground on all sides. The filberts ripen in podlike burrs—without sharp stickers, fortunately—and as soon as they are ripe they fall from the tree and disappear into the thick layer of decomposing leaves and husks that have been accumulating there since the dawn of time. The picker has to search for them amid this mouldering debris. There is little danger of collecting more filberts than you can easily carry. It was a dark and chilly day, and I worked all morning on my knees crawling in and out of the gloomy places under the trees, groping for filberts like a coon hunting tadpoles. By noon I had gathered about five pounds of nuts in my sack. I was discouraged, but since none of the other pickers had done much better, I didn't give up hope.

What awaited us at noon would have been a rude shock, except that a shock implies that something happened. There was no food or drink to be seen anywhere, nor anybody to tell us what to do. We had not expected a free lunch, of course, but we had expected our employer to give a thought to our situation and either sell us something to eat or take us where we could buy a sandwich and a bottle of pop. But the noon hour came and passed while we rested at the edge of the gloomy orchard. There was not even a water bucket. We could not quit, because we were fifteen miles from home and did not know the roads. And there was no one to pay us for our morning's work. So we went back to our dreary job and tried to forget hunger and thirst. I took what satisfaction I could from the thought that I would have my day's pay clear at least, with no expenses for food.

Around five o'clock a straw boss called us out and weighed our sacks of filberts. He used a beam scale hooked up on a tripod and kept his eye on the little brass weights. His manner was hard and busy and he didn't joke and talk. I got the feeling that we were a disappointment to him.

I cannot remember how many pounds of filberts I raked out of the leaves, but I will never forget what I was paid for that day's labor. I can see the coins in my grimy palm—a dime, a quarter, and a fifty-cent piece.

We were too tired to talk during the long bus ride back to the school. When the driver let us out, I walked to the shopping center a block away and spent every cent of my day's pay for a hamburger, a milkshake, and a candy bar. But even that little act of defiant self-indulgence made me feel no better about the events of the day. My good opinion of myself had taken a beating. As a picker, I was obviously a failure. And I had set myself up for my humiliation by being so greedy. I already had a perfectly good paper route and was making more money than I knew what to do with.

I eventually found other lines of work, but that day in the nut orchard taught me a lesson I would never have learned in school. I have a bit of wisdom to pass on to my offspring. "Children," I will say, when they are ready to go out and make their fortunes in the world. "Remember this, because it is the only advice I have for you. *You will never get ahead in the world by picking filberts.*"

A mechanical filbert picker would be something on the order of a cybernetic squirrel. Fortune awaits its inventor, for the sooner the picking trade is wholly mechanized the better.

22 THREE KNIVES

ON THE DESK before me are three old knives, which I keep as mementos and witnesses to the character of the men who once owned and used them. Two are clasp knives—what we call pocketknives—and one has a rigid blade.

The first knife fits my hand comfortably. Its thin black side-pieces cover the metal on both sides, clear out to the rounded ends. Their material looks like plastic but it could be ebony. If it is plastic, it would have to be one of the earlier products like Bakelite. The sidepieces are smooth and shiny. When I rub my fingertip along them I can feel the rounded heads of the three small rivets that hold the knife together. The two at the ends go through the blade tangs and serve as hinge pins when the blades are opened. The third rivet goes through the steel spacer bar below the blade slot.

This knife belonged to William Rogers, my wife's grandfather, whom I know only through her memories and pictures in our album. His Anglo-Irish forebears had followed the frontier from New England across the Alleghenies and into the tall-timbered Ohio Valley, until their westward impulse spent itself in the rich prairies west of the Mississippi.

One of the knife's black sidepieces has a shallow crescent cut into the edge to make it easier to open one of its blades. But the blade with the corresponding fingernail slot is on the other side. There is no way to tell if this is intentional or the result of carelessness when the knife was assembled, for both blades can be opened easily enough.

The blades open at opposite ends, and one is half an inch

longer than the other; otherwise they are identical, with symmetrically pointed ends, like gothic arches. The steel, though tarnished and discolored, shows little sign of wear or resharpening. With a magnifying glass I can make out the letters stamped into the blade tangs. They make the word ULSTER, in block letters less than a sixteenth of an inch high.

It is a thinking man's knife. It would be of almost no use as a weapon. A man driven to desperation, or a man in an uncontrollable rage, might inflict some slight harm with it. But to do so would be to abuse such a civilized and gentlemanly knife.

It is a good knife to open packages with, or to cut string. It would make a good letter opener. You could sharpen a pencil to a fine point with it, clean your golf tees, cut off the tip of a cigar, or clean out your briar pipe. It is an elegant and unpretentious little knife that would not sag noticeably in the pocket of your suit pants. It reflects the values of the genteel tradition, which lasted well up into the twentieth century in some parts of the country.

William Rogers had seen both oceans and the Great Lakes, but his heart never left his home state of Iowa. He owned and edited weekly newspapers in Larchwood and Rock Rapids before the First World War. When a series of bad breaks for which he was not to blame obliged him to find some other way to make a living, he won election to the office of recorder of deeds for Lyon County. Being honest and capable, he became a permanent member of the one-party county government and easily won reelection for the rest of his life.

He lived in Rock Rapids, the county seat, in a two-story white frame house with a yard and a front porch, close enough to the courthouse to walk home for lunch and return at a leisurely pace before one. He had married a girl with the almost incredibly musical-sounding name of Olivia Loveland, and the couple had two children, a boy and a girl, whom they lived to see happily married. In their later years they enjoyed visits from their grandchildren. Mr. Rogers died in his sixties, still holding the office of Lyon County's recorder of deeds.

In 1983 my wife and I went to Rock Rapids, where as a young girl she had often visited her grandparents. It is a town of three or four thousand inhabitants, far up in the most northwestern corner of Iowa. We were there in summer, and it seemed to me that we came to Rock Rapids after driving for miles through a great forest—a forest of corn so high and green and thick that you could not see beyond the first rows alongside the narrow road.

We went to the courthouse where Mr. Rogers had worked for so many years. It is a good example of Midwestern neoclassical architecture, I believe, but it spoke eloquently of virtues that are more Iowan than Greek, reflecting the careful, thrifty integrity of the people who had built it and maintained it for nearly a century. Inside, the halls were cool and quiet, with floors waxed clean and gleaming. A mahogany cap rail on the balustrade around the second-floor rotunda lent warmth to what otherwise might have been too cold and marmoreal a room.

Here was no slovenly indifference to public property. The names and titles on the frosted glass of the doors had no missing letters or peeling paint. The floor of the men's room was laid with small hexagonal marble tiles, clean and white and plain, that had been put down when the walls were going up. And the light switches on the walls were the push-button type set in a brass plate, with one of the buttons capped with mother-of-pearl and the other with black Bakelite. Both buttons were worn down and loose in their sockets, but they worked well.

In the office of the county recorder of deeds, my wife introduced herself to the man and woman behind the wooden divider, who were not busy at the moment. She told them she was a granddaughter of a former county recorder and wanted to look around the office where she had come to meet him and walk home with him for lunch when she was a little girl.

They were the soul of kindness, the recorder and his secretary, and to my wife's delight her grandfather's name was known to them and he was remembered cordially. Not only that—and this is what astonished me—the recorder recalled that a few small items of William Rogers's personal effects had been overlooked at the time of his death and were still in his desk. He rummaged around in the drawers and brought out a small pocket almanac, a knife, a notebook, and another small article or two, which he gave to my wife.

It was as if he had been waiting and expecting somebody to come for those things. But the old gentleman, William Rogers, had been dead for forty years, mind you. My wife was deeply moved, and neither of us could think of anything adequate to say at that moment. But now I would like to say this: they don't throw anything away, in Lyon County, Iowa, and when they build a public building they take good care of it.

The next knife tells a different tale. It is longer and heavier than the black-handled knife, and thicker as well. Its side plates are of horn, cow horn probably—and they are much the worse for wear. The material is cracked and chipped and brown with age. The horn sideplates do not go clear to the ends of the knife but are butted onto steel endpieces welded to the brass shims. These steel ends are rounded and worn smooth. The horn sideplates are fastened on with little rivets of brass. One side has an extra fastener where the horn cracked as the knife was being made.

This knife belonged to my grandfather, Jim Ross, who was born near Mountainburg, in western Arkansas, in the 1860s. His Scotch-Irish forebears had come to this continent so long ago that he had lost any feeling of an overseas origin. Asked where his family was from, he would have replied, "Georgia." He was a big man, over six feet tall, and in the old photos he looks as broad as he was tall. I remember him only in his last years, when hard work and a stroke had confined him to a wheelchair. In his youth he had worked with the men of his family cutting trestle timbers for the first railroads through the Indian Territory. The cut the virgin timber of the Arkansas mountains—tall oaks and ash and hickory trees—hewed them to rough dimensions with axes, and dragged them out of the rough country with horses and log chains to a place where they could load them onto wagons. Rehitching the horses to the wagons, they carted the timbers fifteen or twenty miles to the railroad loading place and stacked them on flatcars, to be taken where they were needed. Enormous amounts of such heavy timber pieces were used to bridge the wide, shallow rivers that meandered across the territory.

My grandfather's old horn-handled knife has three blades. It would be more accurate to say it *had* three blades, for one has been snapped off near the tang. All of the blades bear a trademark stamped into the steel. After sandpapering and cleaning it, I can make out the word SHAPLEIGH in minute letters set around two sides of a little square.

The blades open stiffly and click into their slots with a dull snap. They have been used and resharpened and whetted away until the smaller of the two unbroken blades is a mere sliver of steel. But when both blades are opened to their full extent, you can grasp the horn sidepieces firmly and feel you hold a potent weapon. Though not made for fighting, it is a versatile knife that would stand its owner in good stead on all occasions.

It is a good knife to skin a squirrel with, or to scale fish or castrate hogs. After doing those things, you could wipe the blade on your overalls and cut off a quid of chewing tobacco with it, or peel a peach, or cut up seed potatoes to plant. It is a knife for whittling, for cutting harness leather or shaving down an axe handle. A knife for all seasons, and the seasons have left their mark on it.

I have a group photograph of my timber-cutting Arkansas ancestors. God knows what the occasion was, but it is clear that the men have been forewarned and have dressed for the occasion; that is, they have donned black suit coats over the straps of their overalls. They are all standing stiffly erect and are staring at the photographer from behind their black beards with a grimness that is astonishing. To judge from their expressions they are asking themselves if this picture taker might not have it in mind to run away with their baby sister.

It was customary then for men to be photographed with the tools of their trade, possibly to make them feel more at ease and look more natural. And these men of Arkansas have brought their tools with them. Each man's hands are folded over the end of the handle of a large axe, whose heavy double-bitted blade is grounded at his feet.

Overalls and black coats, broad axes and beards—such things as these do not add up to a gentleman of the old school. And the horn-handled knife is no appurtenance of gentility. Jim Ross was a mountaineer, who married a girl named Liza Stevens, from the highest and farthest-back hills in Arkansas, who bore two sons and four daughters. His westward impulse took his growing family to the Indian Territory and from there to California, then to the state of Washington, and finally back to Missouri. He came back with the Port Arthur Railroad to the tough, half-civilized little towns in the old Cherokee Nation, not far from his first home in Arkansas.

He worked for the railroad, off and on, for much of his life. Not as an engineer (which I, as a child, used to wish) or as a conductor or dispatcher, but first as a laborer on the tracks and later as the foreman of a section gang, responsible for maintaining seventy-five miles of roadbed.

When he retired, the railroad journal printed a piece about him, some of which he wrote himself. Like most men of his background, he was not much of a hand to write, but he could write when he wanted to. So he took pen in hand and told of his first job on the railroad, laying the first lightweight track for the Kansas City Southern (though it had a different name then). He noted the great difference between that first line of track and the track as it was when he retired.

Pride shines through. Pride in the excellence of a first-class railroad, and in being a part of a powerful capitalist enterprise. Those solid lines of heavy-gauge steel, that well-graded and ballasted roadbed with its firmly set cross ties treated with creosote—that was all partly his.

Part of the railroad was *him,* I might say. He never would have said it himself, being innocent of fancy ideas and indifferent to any fine tuning of social justice. So I will say it for him. If the owners—shareholders, capitalists, entrepreneurs, soft-handed men—thought that railroad was all theirs, they were mistaken.

Both of the knives I have described are old—considering the average useful life of such small tools—having been made in the early years of the twentieth century. But the third knife is old beyond any comparison to them. So old that its age can be estimated only in centuries, or even tens of centuries. I found it under thirty inches of loose, dry, wind-deposited dirt on the floor of a bluff shelter high on the side of Coon Mountain. The site is remote and all but inaccessible and cannot be seen from above or below.

I can enclose the knife in the palm of my hand. It is made of a dark gray variety of flint, possibly chert, and has been worked on 100 percent of its surface. In cross section, it is not lens shaped, like most arrowheads, but flatter on one side than the other. One end of the knife is squared, with well-cut corners, and the other end, the blade end, curves to a blunt point. When I hold the knife as if to use it, my thumb fits naturally into a slight depression on the flatter side. This gives a firm grip and allows me to use wrist pressure on the cutting edge.

The edge of the flint blade is sharp, but it is not a tool that would be of much use on wood. The edge of the blade is serrated, so it could not even be used as a scraper of sticks for arrows.

This is a knife to skin a deer with, or even a bear. Once you had slit open the bear's skin, you could peel it back and use the knife to slash the hide free from the fatty connecting tissue. You could use the same knife, after skinning an animal, to cut up its meat, if you knew where to sever the joints and tendons. And if you wanted to tan deerskin or bearskin soft, with all the hair on it, you could use the knife to scrape away the oily scraps of flesh that had come away in the skinning.

So this was the knife of a hunter who camped in the well-protected bluff site with his small band, about the same time perhaps that Viking adventurers first touched the edge of the North American continent. The Cherokees had stopped making flint tools long before they came to what is now Oklahoma. The depth of dirt under which I found the knife tells me that it is without doubt many hundreds of years old. The shelter was too small and difficult of access for a large band to have camped there.

Unlike the first two knives, this one was probably made by the man who used it, one of a small band of hunter-gatherers. What little we know about his time and place leads me to believe that his people had lived for many generations in the broad valley of the Arkansas River. In summer life was easy, and our knife maker could have been up the river and down the river, venturing as far as the open prairie, perhaps, to hunt the great buffalo. Perhaps he had gone down the river with a dugout loaded with deerskins to trade for such things as tobacco.

In the fall, when the leaves had fallen, his band took to the hills and came up the creeks and tributaries to camp near the fresh-water springs, where the woods were full of things to eat. They might stay there through the winter and the spring flood season and return to the river valley when the water subsided.

When I examine the flint knife, one feature of it baffles me. I have seen hundreds of flint artifacts—arrow points and knives and scrapers—and I have found a number of them myself. But I have never seen one quite like this. The base or squared end has a molded look, as if it had been machined rather than chipped into shape. The corner lines have a curve like that where the base shoe of floor molding is joined at a corner.

I can't see how the thing was done. Maybe it was a fluke. But in any case our foraging forebear of pre-Columbian times was more than a hunter and collector of sweet acorns. He was a skilled craftsman who no doubt took some pride in his work and knew an esoteric trick or two when it came to flint.

When he moved on and camped elsewhere, perhaps a day's hard travel away, did he know he had left his knife behind? Did he consider going back to get it? Did he ever intend to return at all? If he gave the matter any thought, could he ever have guessed that his knife would lie there for a thousand years at the hidden campsite in the hills?